antony worrall thompson's

gi diet

with Dr Mabel Blades & Jane Suthering

Photography by Steve Lee

Use the glycaemic index
to find the carbs that will
help you lose weight for
good – with over 100 recipes

Kyle Cathie Ltd

To Janet O'Leary, a beautiful lady who has lived with diabetes all her life but hadn't let it get in the way of enjoyment: a true inspiration to me and many others.

This paperback edition published in Great Britain in 2010 by
Kyle Cathie Limited
23 Howland Street, London, W1T 4AY
www.kylecathie.com

10 9 8 7 6 5 4 3 2 1

ISBN 978-1-85626-947-6

First published in paperback in 2005
Reprinted 16 times

Text © 2005 Dr Mabel Blades
Recipes © 2005 Antony Worrall Thompson, except for Muesli Mix (p46), Apple and Hazelnut Muesli (p46), South African Seed Bread (p52), Fruited Tea Bread (p54) © 2005 Jane Suthering
Photography © 2005 Steve Lee
Book design © 2005 Kyle Cathie Limited

Senior Editor Muna Reyal
Designer Geoff Hayes
Photographer Steve Lee assisted by Tony Briscoe
Home Economist Jane Suthering assisted by Krissy Schmidt
Styling Jo Harris
Copyeditor Morag Lyall
Editorial Assistant Jennifer Wheatley
Recipe Analysis Dr Mabel Blades
Production Sha Huxtable and Alice Holloway

A Cataloguing In Publication record for this title is available from the British Library.

Colour reproduction by Sang Choy
Printed and bound in Singapore by KHL Printing Co.

Contents

introduction

So why, I hear you ask, am I writing about a GI diet? Simple really, a couple of years ago I was diagnosed with Syndrome X or Metabolic Syndrome (a pre-diabetic state) and I was determined to reverse the situation. This meant a total lifestyle change; I always knew I was overweight, I knew I was unfit but I didn't do anything about it, until that is, I was diagnosed with Syndrome X.

The first step was to get my head around the possibility of becoming diabetic. I looked at all the diabetic cookbooks and thought if that is going to be my food life, then I'm finished! I decided to do some research and realised that it was possible for people with diabetes to have enjoyable food after all, so I wrote *Healthy Eating for Diabetes* in 2003.

From there I wanted to go further in my new healthy eating campaign, especially as obesity is becoming a ticking time-bomb in the UK and other Western countries. I undertook to discover a diet that wouldn't be a fad, but would actually be healthy and help you to lose weight at the same time.

Most diets work in the beginning, but almost all are boring so you tend to veer off the straight and narrow very quickly. But as most diets involve reducing the amount of food you eat, your metabolic rate goes down to compensate for the change, so, as soon as you revert to your normal food regime, your body puts on weight more quickly as it has become used to less food.

What we need is a diet regime with a small 'd'. A diet that is so enjoyable it can become part of life's routine. Over the last few years our lives have changed beyond recognition – we've become couch potatoes. Gone is exercise, gone are outdoor pursuits, replaced by computer games, remote controls, DVDs and the like. Similarly with family meals, home cooking has been put on the back burner, we've become content with 'ping' cuisine – mediocre ready meals packed full of preservatives, salt, sugars and fats and heated in the microwave. Or we rely on take-aways, which are, for the most part, equally problematic on the health front.

The time has come to review the modern diet. By not enjoying the social stimulation of family get-togethers around the kitchen table, we lose good food, we lose communication skills, we lose the family unit. Too many of us spend our days eating on the run. Proper breakfast has all but disappeared, lunch comes in the form of sugar-based products, after-work drinks are often sugary alcopops, all of which play havoc with blood sugar levels which, in turn, means energy levels fluctuate. So you have an immediate high after lunch, followed by a crash at about 4pm when you feel exhausted. You reach for something sweet, which will only cause your blood sugar levels to shoot up again, only to come crashing down and so the vicious spiral continues.

My GI diet deals with these issues, providing exciting dishes for you to enjoy; dishes that will remove the feeling that you are on a diet with a big 'D'. There is a huge choice of exciting and varied ingredients available to you and I guarantee that you won't be bored. They are the perfect food for all occasions, and I hope, will give you lots of ideas to generate enthusiasm for a lifestyle change. You will feel better, you will notice improved energy levels and you can live in the knowledge that you have actually found a diet that is good for you, one that is supported by many top nutritionists. Couple this with a bit more exercise and, hey presto, it's a new you.

You can lead a horse to water, but you can't make it drink: your life, your health is down to you. Good luck.

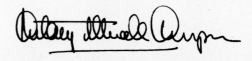

about the gi

there are no bad foods, just bad diets

What we eat is vital to our health and well-being as well as to how we look, feel and function. If we do not feel good then we are not getting the most out of life and not doing all those things we really want to do.

As well as achieving good health, it is essential that we also enjoy our food and feel satisfied by it rather than feeling constantly hungry.

This book is about encompassing that principle by eating foods with a low Glycaemic Index (GI) and low calorie content. Thus it is also about helping people to lose weight and then keep from regaining any weight lost.

Food and dieting

The most important fact to understand is that there are no bad foods, just bad diets with too much fat and sugar and too little fruit and vegetables.

There is nothing wrong with eating a fried breakfast, a cream cake, fish and chips, a bar of chocolate or a packet of potato crisps – provided you only do so occasionally. It is when the whole diet is dominated by these high-fat and high-sugar foods that health problems are likely to occur.

If you divide a plate of food into sections following the recognised guidelines for a balanced diet, there is a place for a small amount of these high-fat and high-sugar foods. So while it is accepted that they provide extra enjoyment and variety to a balanced diet they should not be eaten to excess.

In the same way, you do not have to concentrate your diet solely on low-GI foods, but instead balance your diet by including them where possible. The backbone of this low-GI way of eating is about balance, enjoyment and health.

Unbalanced diets

Unhealthy diets can lead to health problems such as obesity, type 2 diabetes, digestive problems such as irritable bowel

syndrome, cancers and coronary heart disease. The UK Government's Eight Guidelines for a Healthy Diet' are:

- Enjoy your food

- Eat a variety of different foods

- Eat the right amount to be a healthy weight

- Eat plenty of foods rich in starch and fibre

- Eat plenty of fruit and vegetables

- Don't eat too many foods that contain a lot of fat

- Don't have sugary foods and drinks too often

- If you drink alcohol drink sensibly

All these guidelines fit in perfectly with the recipes in this book and will help you to achieve and maintain a sensible weight as well as a nutritionally balanced diet that will help to reduce these health risks.

It matters a great deal that we should take pleasure in our food, purchasing, preparing and then taking the time to savour the meal. This book is about a way of eating that is not only nutritionally balanced, satisfying and low in calories, but also delicious. It is not obsessive about calorie counting or indeed about any type of counting: it is just about healthy and enjoyable eating that you can follow for life, without feeling that you are denying yourself certain foods. The guiding principle behind the GI diet is that you won't even notice that you are on a diet, thus making it much easier to stick to.

One of the problems with many diets that promote weight loss is that they leave you feeling hungry all the time because the allowed portion sizes of carbohydrates are small. As a result you do not feel satisfied and are tempted by snacks and extra portions of foods.

What is different about the GI diet?

Simply put, foods with a low GI are digested more slowly by the body and this helps to keep the blood sugar at a medium level for longer, making us feel satisfied for longer and therefore less hungry. Adding these foods to meals will slow the absorption of the whole meal and thus reduce the GI of the entire meal. This is a brilliant concept because it means that by adding something to a dish then you lower the GI content of the whole meal.

Meals with a low GI are ideal for the whole family as they are easy to incorporate into busy lifestyles as well as family budgets. For children they are particularly satisfying and keep them bursting with energy without continually looking for the next high-fat and high-sugar snack. Meals with a low GI are also nutritionally well balanced, which helps to promote growth. Recent research suggests that low-GI meals help children to avoid gaining excess weight as the food is so satisfying that they do not want the extra high-calorie snacks. For teenagers who are rushing through life at a hectic pace, they provide all the energy they need and keep the blood sugar at a sustained level for longer which helps them to participate in activities be it sport or dancing the night away.

Foods with a low GI are pulses of all types including beans, peas and lentils, whole fruits, oats, grains, bran cereals and multigrain breads, milk and milk products, sweet potatoes, sweetcorn and pasta.

Foods with a medium GI are pitta breads, couscous, boiled potatoes, ice cream, Weetabix and basmati rice.

Foods with a high GI are white and wholemeal bread and flour, biscuits made from them, easy-cook white rice and glucose-based products. These can still be used in dishes provided that they are complemented by ingredients with a low GI.

what is the glycaemic index (gi)?

The GI is really a measure of how our bodies digest, absorb and use different carbohydrate foods to provide energy in the body. Carbohydrate foods, or 'carbs' as they may be referred to today, are sugars and starches. These should be the main source of energy for our bodies.

Our bodies also derive energy from fat but there is a link between obtaining too much energy from fat (especially saturated fat) and coronary heart disease. High-fat diets can be high in calories too and thus contribute to obesity.

Protein foods supply energy to the body as can alcohol, which may account for the fact that a number of overweight men take a large amount of alcohol.

Types of carbohydrates

During the process of digestion carbohydrates are broken down into the component simple sugars or monosaccharides as they are called. The principal one is glucose. This is the tiny molecule that passes through the walls of the intestines and into the bloodstream where it circulates to all the body's cells, which remove the glucose from the blood to provide their energy. Glucose is the main source of energy for all the body's cells.

Sugars other than glucose are called disaccharides and consist of glucose linked with another type of monosaccharide. Sugars such as sucrose, maltose and lactose are made up of half glucose and half another type of monosaccharide. Starches are made up of long chains of glucose molecules.

Foods that contain a high proportion of glucose, such as sweets, release the glucose rapidly into the bloodstream, while those foods that contain disaccharides and starches take longer as the glucose molecules first have to be released from the food being digested.

Carbohydrate foods include

Sugars of all types such as:

● Sucrose or table sugar, whether white or brown, which is found in a number of foods and drinks. Examples of items that contain large amounts of sugar are cakes, jam, pastries, sweets, puddings, chocolates, ice cream, soft drinks; it is also added to teas, coffees and cereals.

● Glucose, which is found in sports drinks and used in syrups and food manufacture.

● Fructose, which is found in fresh fruits and juices made from them as well as processed fruits such as tinned and dried fruits and foods that contain them such as fruit puddings.

● Lactose, which is the sugar found in milk and milk products such as yogurts.

● Maltose, which is found in malt used for flavourings in cereals.

Starches of all types including those found in foods such as:

● Potatoes, rice, pasta, couscous, noodles, breakfast cereals, crackers, grains of all types such as oats and barley.

● Pulses, which include lentils, dried beans and peas, contain substantial amounts of starchy carbohydrate along with proteins.

Various terms are used for starchy carbohydrates, for example, 'unrefined carbohydrates' which refer to those with more fibre such as wholemeal bread, brown pasta, brown rice and wholegrain breakfast cereals.

'Refined carbohydrates' are those that have been more highly processed and have had some of the fibre removed; examples include white bread, white pasta and white rice.

'Starchy carbohydrates' are considered to be the body's preferred source of energy and it is estimated that they should supply about 45–50 per cent of our energy.

Carbohydrates provide 3.75 calories per gram, protein supplies 4 calories per gram and fat 9 calories per gram. Alcohol, if we take it, provides 7 calories per gram. It is therefore clear that a diet high in starchy carbohydrates can be low in calories. Add to this carbohydrates with a low GI and you have a really satisfying way of eating.

How food is used in the body

The food we eat provides us with energy for all our activities such as movement as well as those body functions that we are not aware of, such as maintaining body temperature, providing the energy for body cells, and keeping the heart, lungs and circulation functioning.

Food also provides us with substances such as proteins, which are needed for the repair and growth of body tissues. Food additionally contains minerals such as calcium, required for the maintenance of bones, and vitamins, necessary to regulate the vast array of processes that occurs in the body.

The process of breaking down the food we eat into tiny molecules that our body can absorb is called digestion. Absorption is the process whereby the tiny molecules of nutrients pass across the wall of the digestive tract and into the bloodstream. These nutrients are then carried around the body in the bloodstream and taken up by those parts of the body that require them. Digestion occurs in the digestive tract, or gut as it is sometimes called. Special substances called digestive enzymes are secreted by various parts of the digestive tract and break down foodstuffs into their component parts.

Digestion and absorption occur mainly in the small intestine, but certain simple substances such as glucose and alcohol are absorbed in the stomach. As a result glucose enters the bloodstream rapidly, as does alcohol, which is why we start to feel the effects quickly after drinking it.

When the body has to digest carbohydrate foods that have a tougher coat, such as seeds for example, or take longer to break down because of their structure, then their nutrients take longer to enter the bloodstream. If a food is peeled, mashed or processed before consumption it is easier for the digestive enzymes to attack it and break it down into glucose.

How food affects blood sugar levels

During digestion sugars and starches are broken down into their component parts of glucose.

When glucose is eaten on its own it enters the bloodstream rapidly so that the blood glucose level zooms up quickly. The level also falls quickly; indeed it may dip down very rapidly and to a very low level. That is why we often feel hungry again soon after we have eaten a food that causes a rapid rise in blood glucose level because when we have that equally rapid fall our bodies tell us to eat to boost the blood glucose level up again.

This rise in blood glucose can be measured and this measurement is the basis of the GI. The level to which the blood glucose rises when a set amount of glucose is taken is given a value of 100. Other foods cause different rises in blood glucose level and thus have a different GI (see page 17). Don't worry about these numbers – here the GI index is simplified into low, medium and high GI foods.

Foods with a lower GI tend to make us feel satisfied for longer and thus less inclined to snack. They are broken down slowly in the digestive tract, producing a slow, steady rise and also fall of the blood glucose level, meaning we have a more even release of energy from the food and we feel less hungry.

keeping the gi low

If you add low-GI foods to a meal they mix with foods with a high GI and slow down their digestion and absorption as glucose. So this is a way of eating where you are encouraged to eat more of certain foods.

Many food manufacturers are at present working on studies to find out the different GI levels of the foods they make, but it is fairly straightforward to reduce the GI of meals by mixing a low-GI food with a higher one.

Good examples of this are:

● Serving baked beans with a jacket potato.

● Eating peanut butter on a slice of white toast or wholemeal toast – it is the peanut butter that reduces the GI.

● Using grain and seed breads rather than white or brown breads – it is the hard coatings of the seeds and grains that slow down the digestive process and lower the GI.

● Adding skimmed milk to breakfast cereals – here it is the skimmed milk that lowers the GI.

● Adding extra dried fruit to cake or loaf mixes.

● Having oat biscuits with cheese rather than crackers as the oat biscuits have a lower GI than crackers.

● Serving beans or peas which have a low GI rather than or as well as carrots with a traditional roast.

● Serving more pasta dishes due to the low GI of pasta.

● Adding lentils, barley, butter beans or split peas to your soup to reduce the GI.

● Making a risotto with basmati rice rather than the traditional arborio rice as it has a lower GI.

● Having a snack of dried apricots as well as some sweets.

what should I count?

Foods with a high GI are those with a GI above 70 while those with a medium GI are in the range 56–69 and those with a low GI are 55 or below.

All over the world research projects are being carried out to measure the GI of different foods. However, various factors affect these studies, as the rest of the diet and indeed the previous diet and health status of the participants can affect the GI. And some of the values vary, especially between different brands.

Some researchers suggest using the 'Glycaemic Loads' of foods rather than the GI. This is the GI multiplied by the amount of carbohydrate in a food. Others have used a GI point system, which is a relationship between the GI and the energy density of a food.

To achieve weight loss a calorie reduction is needed and some people therefore advocate counting calories. Counting, listing and adding up numbers may suit some people but for most it becomes a chore and they soon give up. Sometimes, too, people get it wrong.

So this way of eating is based on the simple principles of a low-GI and low-calorie diet.

Portion sizes

The one thing that you should try to keep an eye on is portion size.

To lose weight, the portion sizes should be kept to about 100g (3½oz) for meats, 100–150g (3½–5oz) for fish, 50g (2oz) for nuts, 25g (1oz) for cheese, 1–2 eggs per portion at mealtimes and 500ml or just under a pint of skimmed milk per day.

It is boring to be obsessive about portion sizes but try to check their weights on scales or when you buy foods so that you begin to recognise what these foods weigh.

the gi food table

Foods with a low GI

So which carbohydrate foods have a low GI?

Breads, breakfast cereals and cereals
All-bran
Barley
Buckwheat
Bulgur wheat
Grain breads
Oat bran
Oats
Pasta of all types
Pumpernickel
Rice noodles
Seeded breads
Sourdough rye
Soya and linseed bread
Spelt wheat bread
Toasted muesli
Turkish wholewheat bread

Vegetables and pulses
Baked beans
Black-eye beans
Butter beans
Chickpeas
Haricot beans
Kidney beans
Lentils
Lima beans
Small new potatoes boiled in skin
Peas
Soya beans
Sweet potatoes
Sweetcorn

Fruits
Apples
Bananas
Cherries
Dried apples
Dried apricots
Grapefruit and its juice
Grapes
Kiwi fruit
Mangoes
Oranges
Peaches
Pears
Plums
Prunes
Strawberries

Snack foods
Apple juice
Cashew nuts
Corn chips
Cranberry juice
Hot chocolate
Grainy fruit loaf
Low-fat chocolate mousse
Low-fat custard
Low-fat yogurt
Malted milk
Minestrone soup
Peanuts
Skimmed milk
Tomato soup
Tortillas (corn and wheat)

Foods with a medium GI

A number of foods are considered to have a medium GI.

Breads, breakfast cereals and cereals
Arborio rice
Arrowroot biscuits
Basmati rice
Brown rice
Chapati
Couscous
Croissants
Crumpets
Gnocchi
Hamburger buns
Melba toast
Pancakes
Pitta bread
Rice noodles
Rye crispbreads
Wholemeal rye bread

Vegetables and pulses
Beetroot
Carrots
Potatoes, peeled and boiled

Fruits
Dried figs
Melon
Pineapple
Tinned apricots
Tinned fruit cocktail
Tinned peaches

Snack foods
Bean soup
Digestive biscuits
Flans
Ice cream
Muesli bars
Muffins
Oatmeal biscuits
Pea soup
Plain cake
Potato crisps
Raisins

Foods with a high GI

Includes glucose and foods that contain glucose.

Breads, breakfast cereals and cereals	*Fruits*
Baguettes	Dates
Bagels	Tinned lychees
Bread stuffing	Watermelon
Coco pops	
Corn pops	*Snack foods*
Crackers	Corn cakes
Crunchy nut cornflakes	Doughnuts
Dark rye bread	French fries – frozen and
Gluten-free bread	re-heated
Gluten-free maize pasta	Fruit bars
Gluten-free rice	Glucose tablets
Jasmine white rice	Honey
Puffed wheat	Jelly beans
Rice crackers	Morning coffee biscuits
Rice krispies	Plain scones
Shredded wheat	Popcorn
Sultana bran	Pretzels
Tapioca	Rice cakes
White bread	Glucose-based drinks,
White rice	e.g. sports drinks
Wholemeal bread	Tofu desserts
	Wafer biscuits
Vegetables and pulses	Waffles
Broad beans	
Jacket potatoes	
Mashed potato	
Parsnips	
Pumpkins	
Swede	

Fats, protein and GI

Because fats and protein foods are not made up of glucose units, it means that they all have a GI of 0. Adding a low-GI food to meals can reduce the overall GI of the meal as it mixes with the other foods and slows down digestion and absorption.

This means that adding oils, fats and cream to dishes reduces the GI of a meal. However, adding more fat to meals means that their calorie value shoots up and if too many calories are eaten then weight is gained rather than lost.

Nonetheless the concept of adding something to meals to reduce the GI can be promoted: using small amounts of fats and oils for cooking and for spreading on bread can be helpful as well as adding extra flavour.

Other foods such as those that supply protein not only balance a meal from a nutritional point of view but also reduce the GI. Therefore eating these foods as part of a meal will actually reduce the GI (but note portion sizes – see page 17):

● Skimmed milk or semi-skimmed milk has a low-GI value because it contains the milk sugar lactose

● Eggs

● Very low-fat cheeses

● Low-fat yogurts

● Lean meats such as beef, pork and lamb as well as their livers and kidneys

● Poultry such as chicken and turkey without skin

● Game such as hare, rabbit, pigeon and pheasant

● Fish and shellfish of all types

● Nuts of all types and nut spreads such as peanut butter

how the gi can help

Diabetes

Diabetes is a common disorder whereby the body does not produce enough insulin or produces ineffective insulin, which the body requires to enable all its cells to take up glucose. There are two types of diabetes:

Type 1 where the pancreas stops producing insulin: this type of diabetes affects mainly children and younger people. It usually has a rapid onset with severe symptoms such as weight loss; excessive thirst and even coma can develop. This type of diabetes needs insulin for treatment.

Type 2 which mainly affects older people and those who are overweight. The onset is often very slow and many people are found to have type 2 diabetes after having a routine medical or even an eye test. The symptoms tend to vary and be less acute than those for type 1 diabetes. Symptoms include thirst, passing urine frequently and tiredness.

Whichever the type of diabetes, the blood glucose level rises above the normal level as the production of insulin is not working properly. Altering the diet to maintain a lower blood glucose level is therefore fundamental to control the condition.

Thus an eating pattern where low-GI foods are included enables the blood sugar level to be well controlled and assists in the long-term management of diabetes. Many of those with type 2 diabetes are overweight, so eating a low-calorie, low-GI diet is brilliant for promoting weight loss and hence long-term control of the diabetes.

Good control of the blood glucose level means that diabetes sufferers have a reduced risk of developing any of the complications associated with the condition.

Syndrome X

This is considered to be a metabolic disorder that could lead to future heart problems, type 2 diabetes, strokes and diseases that affect the blood vessels and circulation. At present it is thought that this condition is very common and probably affects a quarter of those over 20 years of age and half of those over 50.

Syndrome X is associated with abdominal fat deposition which results in a waist that is nearly as large or larger than the hips giving the so-called apple shape (see also page 24). It is also linked with low levels of the protective cholesterol in the blood and high levels of another sticky substance called triglycerides circulating in the blood. Also insulin resistance, where the insulin does not work correctly, occurs which causes raised levels of blood glucose. High blood pressure levels are also found.

Doctors or nurses can offer tests for all these factors. However, a diet rich in low-GI foods will help to maintain low blood sugar levels, while a low-calorie diet for weight loss will help to control Syndrome X.

Digestive disorders and IBS

Many people suffer from digestive and bowel problems such as irritable bowel syndrome (IBS). Eating adequate amounts of foods that are slowly digested, and which also contain fibre and are low in fat, accompanied by drinking adequate amounts of fluid greatly assists those with bowel problems such as IBS.

Foods with a low GI are beneficial in promoting a healthy flora of bacteria in the bowel and intestines, which reduces bloating, bowel disorders and also food sensitivities.

Other health problems helped by low-GI meals

A number of other health problems are helped by a diet with a low GI. Such disorders include:

Polycystic ovary syndrome where the maintenance of the blood glucose level can help to control symptoms and aid weight loss.

Coronary heart disease and raised lipid levels in the blood are assisted by a diet that maintains the blood sugar level without the peaks and troughs found in a diet with high-GI foods. This diet is also low in fats and therefore helps to prevent coronary heart disease.

Hypoglycaemia, with the repeated low blood sugar level and symptoms of shakiness that occur, is helped by the maintenance of the blood sugar level which results when a low-GI diet is followed.

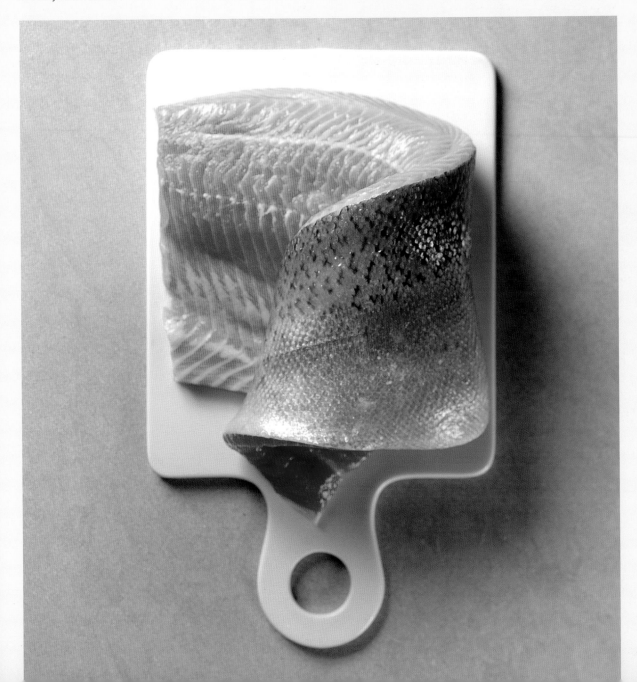

weight loss and the gi

As the concept of GI is fairly new there are few studies on it, but those there are show that it is helpful in promoting a slow, steady weight loss with no hunger pangs.

Long-term weight loss

There is no point in losing weight just to put it back on again. Indeed it is unhealthy for your weight to yo-yo up and down.

All too often people regard diets as short term. This one is not a diet for a short time but an improved way of eating that can be sustained for life and in all situations, so that any weight lost remains lost!

This way of eating has no forbidden foods, just a healthy diet with extras of low-GI foods to sustain a healthy blood sugar level.

Being overweight

The weight that anyone who is overweight needs to lose is fat. Most people would love to lose it quickly and indeed at many slimming groups those who lose the most weight each week are applauded and rapid weight loss is celebrated.

A rapid weight loss may well be due to a loss of fluid and muscle as well as fat. This is likely to result from a strict diet, which means there is no education in eating habits. So when the diet is given up any weight lost returns – and usually with a bit extra. If muscle tissue is lost then it is often replaced with more fat, which is an unhealthy type of tissue.

Quite honestly, as a dietitian dealing with someone who has been overweight for a long time my goal is first to stop the person continuing to gain weight and then to maintain their weight for a few weeks. This gives them confidence not only for a long-term weight loss but also for maintaining a new low weight when that is achieved. Next I encourage a slow, steady weight loss of 450g–1kg (1–2¼lb per week). This

In the developed world over half of the population is overweight or obese. Many people are concerned about their weight and move from one sort of diet to another, which means they veer from one type of eating to another with the consequence that weight is lost and then regained, often with more besides.

This book will help those who are overweight to lose weight by following a diet that is low in GI as well as low in calories. It enables readers to reduce the GI level of their foods and thus helps them to feel more satisfied after eating. The recipes are inspirational and give a tempting array of calorie-counted dishes (as well as being low in fat and salt) that can be included in a low-calorie diet to bring about sensible weight loss that can be maintained.

This way of eating thus becomes enjoyable and can be maintained not just for weeks or months, but long-term.

means that body fat is being shed and also the person is gradually adjusting their diet into their ordinary lifestyle, making it easier to keep to the new eating pattern.

Not only can they keep to the new eating pattern but they can also enjoy feeling full, and fit the major principles of the new way of eating into family meals, eating out, parties and the general rush of twenty-first-century living.

How it happens

The basic reason why people become overweight is that they consume too many calories from food for their own individual needs. They then store these calories up as fat both under the skin and around the vital organs.

It is so easy to be tempted to eat more than we need with the readily available range of foods everywhere we go. In an age when everyone is extremely busy with work, home life and travelling to and from places it is difficult to find enough time to buy and prepare meals. Also, many people are unsure about what to buy for a well-balanced diet and how to cook various foods. Thus any hunger pangs are easily satisfied by grabbing a quick snack on the way to work, another from the trolley at mid-morning, a fast-food lunch fitted in between shopping, chocolate and potato crisps bought on the way home as we fill up with petrol, a quick and easy microwave dinner containing few vegetables and then snacks in the evening between chores. All the time we are snacking these highly processed foods our blood glucose level will be bouncing up and down, making us feel continually hungry and continuing the cycle.

Constantly eating high-calorie snacks means we keep up the vicious cycle of piling on weight because it becomes more difficult to make the effort involved to eat properly.

Problems associated with being overweight
As anyone who is overweight knows there are a number of issues that have to be faced on an everyday basis. These include the sinking feeling when clothes do not fit anymore and we feel that we are not as healthy as we once were. Stairs become more of an issue as rushing up them causes breathlessness, so we take the lift and therefore expend fewer calories. People who are overweight may also feel self-conscious about their bodies and so may be less inclined to undertake any sport or activity that demands revealing clothing such as a swimming costume or shorts and as a result take less exercise.

They are also less likely to have self-confidence: many overweight people are locked into a cycle of poor self-esteem which affects their relationships, career, activities and how they look after themselves – for example, many will not spend much on their appearance and plan to do so only when they have lost weight. Many of my really obese patients are almost housebound because of their sheer bulk.

There are obviously many health problems associated with being overweight and these include:

● Coronary heart disease

● Type 2 diabetes

● Joint problems such as arthritis and back problems

● Certain types of cancers

● High blood pressure

● Slower recovery from surgery

● Depression

● Fertility problems

● Gallstones

● Breathing difficulties

How 'overweight' is measured

There are various ways of measuring obesity. The ones commonly seen are the height/weight charts, which show a relationship between weight and height and suggest ideal weights.

More recently Body Mass Indexes (BMIs) have been used, which are a more complex relationship between height and weight. To work out your BMI, take your weight in kilograms and divide it by the square of your height, measured in metres (BMI = weight in kg $\div$ height in metres^2). Fortunately there are charts that show BMIs and make individual calculations unnecessary. The BMIs are categorised into various levels, which show the associated health risks:

A BMI below 20 signifies someone being underweight.

A BMI between 20 and 25 is the normal weight range at which there are few health risks.

A BMI between 26 and 30 signifies the range where someone is regarded as being overweight.

A BMI between 30 and 40 is the range regarded as obese and associated with numerous health risks.

A BMI above 40 signifies someone being severely obese and is strongly associated with health problems.

Often moving from one BMI category to a lower one motivates people to lose weight and thus reduce their health risks. Despite metrication, however, many people only know their weight in stones and pounds and find its equivalent in kilos meaningless.

The worst place for anyone to deposit fat is around the waist and middle area – the so-called apple shape, as opposed to the pear shape, where weight is deposited around the hips.

A good and effective measure of overweight and obesity is therefore to measure the waist. Generally men should have a waist measurement of below 94cm (37in) and women a measurement of below 80cm (31in). This is quick and easy to do and needs only a tape measure.

Calorie content of meals

Calories are the units for the measurement of energy and apply both to the energy content of foods as well as that energy expended in activities.

In general an adult man needs about 2,500 calories per day and a woman 2,000 calories. To lose weight we need to take in fewer calories than we expend so that the fat stores in the body are burnt up for our energy needs.

Reducing calorie intake
It is best to make only small adjustments initially and try to keep to around 1,500 calories per day for women wanting to lose weight and 2,000 calories per day for men.

A pound of fat contains about 3,500 calories so to lose this amount of weight in a week a reduction of 3,500 calories is needed. Therefore if the calorie content of a diet is adjusted down by about 500 calories per day, this level of weight loss will be achieved.

Keep to this reduction of about 500 calories per day and at the same time increase exercise levels. As you become fitter it is easy to increase the amount of exercise taken. Thus weight loss is continued. Only reduce the amount of calories further if you have not lost any weight for three to four weeks.

Such a reduction is actually quite easy to do, as only small adjustments have to be made to your diet, such as reducing the amount of spreads put on bread, swapping some of the high-fat and high-sugar snacks for fruit and snacks with a low GI, avoiding fried foods and high-fat items such as creamy sauces and pastries. Introducing Antony's recipes into your diet will ensure your meals are low in GI and calories.

The recipes in this book are all below 300 calories per portion when weight loss is wanted and below 500 calories where weight maintenance is desired (marked by a green semicircle with +300 inside).

While it can be tedious for some people to write down everything they eat, others find it helpful – so do which you prefer. However, one invaluable tip is to plan a week's menus based on ideas and recipes from this book so that you have something to look forward to and can plan shopping trips for ingredients accordingly.

If you have a period when you find reducing the calorie level difficult, for example over the Christmas season, do not get disheartened, just go back to the main principles of the diet as soon as life permits.

Exercise

Exercise strengthens the muscles including the heart, which is after all just a muscle, and thus some type of exercise needs to be taken to promote weight loss. Exercise results in an increase in energy expenditure that will help to burn up calories and achieve a greater loss than the 500-calorie reduction each day alone. This means that diet is not your only means of losing weight.

Our lifestyle today tends to reduce daily activity levels and it is the little things that add up to make a difference to them. Think of the inventions that have caused a reduction in daily energy expenditure today: using duvets rather than walking around the bed to tuck in sheets and blankets; using dryers rather than pegging out washing; using remote controls instead of having to get up to switch channels on TV; and using cases with wheels rather than having to carry them.

To try to increase exercise levels on a daily basis initially means making several small changes: use the stairs; get up and stand when answering the phone; walk rather than drive, get off the bus one stop early. Most effective is to walk more and take more regular exercise.

Ideally, you should take 30 minutes of exercise each day, sustained for at least 10 minutes at a time. Going to a gym, doing classes for different exercises, dancing, playing team sports and swimming are all excellent, but many people find that with a busy lifestyle they do not have time to fit such activities into their schedule.

Walking is therefore an ideal exercise that most people can incorporate into their day. I find two ways helpful to encourage walking:

First I often urge people to buy a pedometer and to wear this and measure the number of steps they take in a day. Some of the very inactive ones only take about 1,500 but they then try to improve on their own levels by taking 1,510 the next day and so on until they reach the recommended 10,000 steps per day.

The second way that I encourage people to walk is to ask them to go out of their door and walk for five minutes and then to turn around and try to get home in less than five minutes. This is such a quick and easy way of doing extra walking that many find it fun and take children and partners with them.

Stress and relaxation

When they are stressed some people comfort eat and are less likely to motivate themselves into taking exercise. Therefore it is important for everyone to build some time for relaxation into their schedule. This relaxation may be achieved in many ways, even by exercise or going for a walk. Often just getting outside into the fresh air is in itself relaxing.

Other forms of relaxation can be formalised using relaxation techniques of clearing the mind and slowing down breathing rates; or they can be something as simple as browsing around the shops, stroking the cat, reading, listening to music or even playing with the children.

nutrition

This is an absolutely fascinating subject with research appearing all the time with new information about the actions of foods in the body as well as different substances found in foods. The whole area of GI is relatively new but one that is based on good scientific analysis of foods.

Unfortunately nutrition abounds with various terms and abbreviations, which are often irrelevant to everyday eating. People put foods together as meals, and factors other than nutritional content come into play when eating.

The concept of the GI and low-calorie foods can be based on straightforward principles about foods and suggestions of different combinations of foods to eat rather than on complex calculations. This means that the diet can be easily adopted and become a long-term way of eating which encompasses all the realities of life such as holidays and meals out.

Energy

All foods provide us with energy and eating too much of any of them can make us gain weight. However, if foods are really satisfying, such as those carbohydrates with a low GI, it is difficult to eat very large amounts of them.

As already mentioned, energy is measured in calories, the term most commonly known, or kilocalories; the metric measurement is joules.

Carbohydrates are the least concentrated source of energy so they are brilliant for filling up on. Fats, and foods containing them in quantity, are a more dense energy source than carbohydrates and can also be easily eaten in large amounts, thus forming the basis of a high-calorie diet. Alcohol must be taken into account in the overall calorie intake and failure to do so may well lead to weight gain.

Some carbohydrate foods such as sugars supply 'empty calories' which means that they do not supply any nutrients other than calories.

Carbohydrate and fibre

Carbohydrate foods with a low GI are those that are slowly broken down into the component glucose molecules, which are then absorbed. If the carbohydrates are associated with dietary fibre, such as skins, pips and seeds, then this slows down the digestive process and their absorption.

Dietary fibre used to be called roughage but is now correctly called non-starch polysaccharide or NSP. Too little dietary fibre is linked with a number of health problems including diverticular disease, bowel cancer and constipation. We are advised to take about 18g (¾oz) of dietary fibre each day but on average we have only 12g (just over ½oz) so it is little surprise that we see an increase in these problems.

The two types of dietary fibre

The first is soluble fibre, which is smooth and viscous and is found in foods such as oats, barley and pulses (peas, beans and lentils) as well as in fruit and vegetables. This type of fibre is associated with slowing down digestion in the small intestine and moderating blood sugar and blood cholesterol levels. This is the fibre found in many foods with a low GI, which is why they have beneficial effects on the blood glucose level.

The second type is insoluble fibre which adds bulk in the bowel by holding onto water and this is the type associated with bran, wholemeal cereals, wholemeal flour, brown pasta and brown rice.

Both types of fibre are valuable but the soluble fibre, and thus many of the carbohydrate foods with a low GI, is particularly useful for those with diabetes and raised cholesterol levels.

Fruit and vegetables

It is recommended that we all eat five portions of fruit and vegetables per day. (That is fruit and vegetables combined, not five portions of each.) However if we can manage more than the five portions that is really good news, as most fruit and vegetables have a low GI.

These five portions are based on the World Health Organisation's recommendation that we should eat 400g (14oz) of fruit and vegetables each day for the health benefits they provide. Unfortunately, in Britain, despite this encouragement, on average we consume only three portions.

The term fruit and vegetables includes all types with the exception of potatoes, which are considered to be a starchy carbohydrate food, as are plantains or green bananas.

It should also be noted that as leafy green vegetables such as lettuce, cabbage, broccoli and sprouts all contain little carbohydrate, they have a negligible GI.

So what is a portion of fruit or vegetables?

Half a large fruit such as a grapefruit.

One medium-sized fruit such as a medium apple, pear, banana or peach.

One teacup of small fruits such as cherries, damsons or grapes.

A slice of melon, pineapple or mango – each about 2.5cm (1in) wide.

Two small fruits such as plums.

One tablespoon of dates or dried apricots or sultanas or one of the small matchbox-size packs of dried fruits.

Three tablespoonfuls of tinned or stewed fruit.

Two tablespoonfuls of cooked, frozen or tinned vegetables. This equates to 80g (3oz) of vegetables. If this is a pulse vegetable such as peas, beans or lentils it only counts as one portion no matter how much is eaten in a day.

A bowl of salad.

A small glass or carton of fruit juice. Fruit juice counts as only one portion no matter how much is drunk in a day.

Many fruits such as grapefruit, cherries, mangoes, oranges, peaches, pears, grapes and plums have a low GI, as can be seen from the list on page 18, and are therefore a valuable addition to meals. A further plus is that fruit is low in calories.

But even fruit with a relatively high GI such as melon is low in calories and useful to add to any diet. Dates, despite their high GI, can be used for sweetening and are much more beneficial than white sugar.

Fruit is a source of vitamins that act as powerful antioxidants, which have a protective effect on the immune system of the body and are associated with lower levels of cancers and coronary heart disease.

To keep the GI value of fruit and vegetables as low as possible eat them unpeeled and cook in chunks rather than mashing or puréeing them. In this way the digestive process has to work harder and the GI level is lowered.

Dairy foods

Dairy foods such as milk and yogurt and foods made from milk such as milk shakes and custards are all excellent sources of calcium in the diet. Because milk contains the sugar lactose they also have a low GI value. These foods are relatively low in calories and can be used to advantage in reducing the GI while adding that all-important source of calcium.

Calcium is important for bone health and we need a regular intake. Other sources are hard cheeses, which have a GI of 0 but which are relatively high in calories due to the fat content. Fish with bones are another source of calcium.

To keep the calorie level of the diet low choose skimmed milk, low-fat cheeses such as Edam or use only small portions of full-fat cheeses. Eat diet yogurts and low-fat fromage frais to keep the calorie level down. For those who take soya milk or rice milk it is important to choose one with added calcium.

Full fat milk contains 3.9 per cent fat, semi-skimmed milk 1.6 per cent fat and fully skimmed milk 0.1 per cent fat. Children up to the age of 2 should be given full fat milk and semi-skimmed milk can be introduced thereafter. Skimmed milk can be given to children from 5 years of age.

Vegetarian and vegan diets

Anyone following a vegetarian or vegan diet often has a head start in reducing the GI of their meals as they tend to use more low-GI foods such as pulses, nuts and seeds.

For vegetarians, eggs and milk as well as vegetarian cheese can be included, which will provide protein. Meat is a major source of iron so excluding it means that an alternative source such as pulses or nuts or products made from them should be taken. The iron in meat is in the haem form, similar to the haemoglobin that circulates in our blood, so it is well absorbed, while that from plant sources is in the non-haem form and is poorly absorbed. Vitamin C, which is found in fruit and vegetables, aids the absorption of non-haem iron.

Fats

There are various types of fats but whether saturated, polyunsaturated or monounsaturated, all fats provide 9kcal per gram and are thus equal as a source of energy. Too much energy in the diet can contribute to weight gain and for health it is recommended that we should obtain no more than 35 per cent of energy from the fat in the diet.

Although fats have a GI of 0 and can therefore reduce the overall GI of a meal or dish, adding fat is not a good way of manipulating the GI as it adds extra unwanted calories.

Saturated fats

These are derived from animal sources such as full-cream milk and cheese, lard, butter, coconut cream, the fat found on meat and other fatty foods such as pastry. They are less desirable because they have been linked with coronary heart disease.

Polyunsaturated fats

Polyunsaturated fats are derived from plant oils such as soya and corn. These oils are thought to be beneficial, particularly to heart health, but still provide a source of calories.

Essential fatty acids

Omega-3 fatty acids can help prevent blood clotting so they are particularly helpful in preventing coronary heart disease. They are also helpful in preventing inflammation and thus may be beneficial in joint diseases. Sources of omega-3 fatty acids are fish oils, particularly those from oily fish such as salmon, trout, pilchards, mackerel and sardines.

These special fatty acids are also found in linseeds and soya beans – both of which have a low GI and are perfect for adding to salads and casseroles.

Omega-6 fatty acids can help prevent coronary heart disease as they reduce levels of the harmful LDL cholesterol. Sources of omega-6 fatty acids are sunflower oil, corn oil and soya oils.

Monounsaturated fats

Monounsaturated fats are found in olive oil and rapeseed oil and are considered to be beneficial to the heart.

Trans fats

Most natural fats contain cis bonds. This cis bond is the way in which the chemical elements in the fatty acids are joined together. However in manufacturing margarines and shortenings, which are used in manufacturing biscuits and cakes, the polyunsaturated fats are hydrogenated and more trans fatty acid bonds are formed as the cis bonds are broken and reformed in the trans form.

These trans fatty acids are considered to be similar to saturated fats in their effect on health and are linked with coronary heart disease.

Cholesterol

This is a sticky wax-like substance. It is vital for life and is involved in making essential substances in the body such as cell membranes and hormones. Cholesterol circulates in the blood in two forms and can indicate a risk of coronary heart disease. There are two types of cholesterol:

Low density lipoprotein cholesterol (LDL): the more harmful type of cholesterol

High density lipoprotein cholesterol (HDL): the beneficial type of cholesterol

A high proportion of saturated fat in the diet predisposes the production of the more harmful type of cholesterol. Some foods such as liver, egg yolks and shellfish are naturally a source of cholesterol. There is no need for most people to avoid these nutritious foods but anyone who has high levels of the harmful type of cholesterol may have been advised to limit their consumption of them.

Fluid

Fluid is absolutely essential to health and it is important to take sufficient fluid each day. Ideally we should have 2 litres (3½ pints); that is about eight cups or glasses of fluid each day. The preferred fluid to rehydrate the body is water.

About 70 per cent of the body is fluid and all the vital actions that occur in the body take place in a liquid environment. Adequate fluid is especially needed for the digestive processes to function properly. A lack of fluid can result in numerous problems including tiredness and irritability.

Sometimes it seems to me when dealing with overweight people that they think they are hungry and eat rather than recognise the body's signals of thirst. The amount of fluid they consume is very low but the number of snacks disproportionately very high. Thus they never feel properly satisfied. In some individuals, just getting them to drink more seems to curtail their appetite for snacks.

Teas, coffees and colas are useful to add variety but most are a source of caffeine, which acts as a diuretic and makes the body lose fluid. Avoid adding sugar to drinks and also choose low-calorie or sugar-free drinks rather than those that contain sugar, which will add extra calories.

Fruit juices are relatively high in calories and are best diluted with water. Sugary drinks also have a high GI.

Alcohol

Alcohol can provide a pleasant and relaxing extra to many people's daily intake. There is nothing wrong with this; indeed a little alcohol, especially red wine, each day is considered to be beneficial to heart health.

As regards health, alcohol is measured in units with 1 unit of alcohol being equivalent to a glass of wine, single pub measure of spirits, half a pint of beer, lager or cider, and a small schooner of sherry. Many of the stronger beers and spirit-based mixer drinks contain 2 or more units per serving.

The government recommendations as regards alcohol are for women to have not more than 21 units per week and for men not more than 28 units per week. This does not mean that you can save up the whole week's units and take them as a binge one single evening as this can have disastrous effects on health.

As regards calories in alcohol, a half pint of beer provides about 90–120 calories, a small glass of wine about 70 calories and some of the 'alcopop' and mixed drinks between 150 and 200 calories per bottle, so the calories soon add up.
Try to ensure any mixers are of the low-calorie type. Also have a glass of water for every glass of alcohol taken, to limit the intake and also reduce the adverse effects that alcohol has on hydration.

Excess alcohol is linked with liver cirrhosis and provides extra calories. It is recommended that we all have an alcohol-free day per week to allow the liver cells to regenerate.

Salt

At present we take an average of 9–12g of salt per person per day when we actually only need about 6g. Salt is made up of sodium and chloride with about 1g of sodium in 2.5g of salt. Sodium has a harmful effect on blood pressure. 6g of salt contains about 2.5g of sodium.

Salt is particularly found in manufactured foods such as tinned soups, tinned vegetables and meals; it is also found in savoury snacks such as potato crisps and salted peanuts. Foods such as cheese, bacon and ham and salted fish contain salt, where it is used as a preservative. Sodium is also found in monosodium glutamate, which is used as a flavour-enhancer in manufactured foods such as ready meals.

Fresh food such as fruit and vegetables as well as meat, milk and eggs are all low in sodium. It is best to use a minimum of salt, and gradually reducing the amount of salt in both cooking and sprinkled on food can allow the taste buds to change and become accustomed to less salt.

In general the recipes in this book contain a low level of salt i.e. below 0.5g per portion. However ingredients such as cheese, shellfish, bacon, ham, tinned vegetables, soy sauce, black pudding, sausages and fish sauce all contain salt which is required for their preservation and production. Therefore recipes containing these ingredients will have a higher level of sodium. Choose low sodium options such as light soya sauce, low-salt stock cubes and beans tinned in water where possible.

Although it is important to keep salt levels low, remember that this is a salt intake averaged over a period of days so the odd higher salt recipe can be balanced out by a low salt one.

Vitamins and mineral supplements

These are the micronutrients that are needed in tiny amounts – some as little as millionths of a gram – but which are essential to keep us healthy. If we eat a wide variety of foods then we are likely to get everything we need in our diet.

food labelling

A low-GI diet focuses on lots of fresh and simple foods and thus contains a range of vitamins and minerals. However, with rushed and skipped meals as well as an occasional prevalence of highly processed foods we may not get as well balanced an intake of vitamins as we should.

Some groups such as women who wish to become pregnant or who are in the early stages of pregnancy are recommended to take a supplement of folic acid.

For those who follow a vegan way of eating their diet can be low in iron or vitamin B12 (meat is a major source of iron, and vitamin B12 is found in foods such as meat, fish, milk and eggs). Vitamin B12 is also found in yeast products and if these are not taken then vegans may need a supplement.

People following a milk-free diet may be at risk of not taking enough calcium and supplements can be useful here. For other people a multi-vitamin and mineral supplement may be beneficial each day if their diet is erratic at times.

The manufacturers of processed foods are required by law to list the ingredients they contain in descending order of quantity. Reading a food label can produce a few surprises when you find that the fish pie contains sugar and the tin of carrots an amount of salt and colouring.

Many labels provide nutritional information and now some food labels are giving information on the GI. This usually indicates that a food has a low, medium or high GI content.

Food labels contain information on food additives and these items are usually towards the bottom of the list of ingredients as they tend to be present in tiny amounts. Without the use of additives and food preservation techniques we could not easily have our present lifestyle, but we should try to minimise our intake.

By following a low-GI diet and eating more fruit and vegetables – which are fresh and therefore unlabelled – you will soon reduce the overall level of additives in the diet.

low gi tips

Low-GI meals

To follow this way of eating there is no need to be obsessive: just try to reduce the GI content of some of the carbohydrate foods you eat.

Main meals

Curries made with chickpeas and lentils

Pasta dishes served with sauces containing meat or beans and lots of vegetables and tomatoes instead of cream

Stir-fries with lots of vegetables, beans and peas

Use basmati rice

Use beans in as many dishes as possible, such as chillis

Puddings

Chunky fruit salads

Compôtes made with dried fruits

Crumbles that include oats

Fresh fruits

Ice cream and fruits

Milk puddings

How to reduce the GI content of a day's menu

There are quite a few easy changes you can make to reduce the GI of a day's menu.

Breakfast can include porridge, grapefruit, a low-GI cereal with skimmed milk, toasted seeded bread spread with peanut butter, a cooked breakfast (grilled lean bacon and low-fat sausages and poached eggs) served with baked beans, kedgeree made with basmati rice.

Lunch can include a jacket potato with baked beans, seeded bread or rolls with lentil soup, sandwiches using seeded bread, baked beans on toast, bean and pasta salads, pitta breads filled with salad.

The main meal can include roasted meats or baked fish served with large amounts of vegetables especially beans and new potatoes cooked in their skins, casseroles that include beans and chickpeas, pasta dishes served with extra vegetables and tomato sauces.

Low GI for the family

This is such a simple way of eating that the family will probably not notice that the foods have a low GI. It is ideal for all family members as the meals are sustaining and satisfying and mean that everyone can get on with enjoying life rather than seeking out the next snack.

For children it is an especially good way of eating as it fills them up and thus stops them continually wanting sugary and salty snacks. Also the moderated and sustained blood sugar level may help concentration levels – and behaviour.

Unfortunately many children are overweight these days and there are preliminary suggestions that a low-GI diet helps to prevent this.

For many elderly people the low-GI meals are evocative of traditional dishes containing more grains and pulses.

Shopping

When shopping for low-GI foods look for fresh and dried fruit vegetables and pulses. Many people worry about soaking and cooking dried beans. If you are concerned invest in lots of tins of these beans both for quickness and convenience. But do buy a pack of dried lentils, as they are so easy to cook and have a very low GI. They do not require soaking, take only 15 minutes to cook and make a wonderful addition to curries and casseroles.

● Any dried beans or split peas and cereals like barley have a very low GI and the dried ones, when home-cooked, result in a final dish with a lower GI than if tinned varieties are used.

● Look for seeded bread, or make your own in a bread maker, which is so easy to do. You can buy packs of seeds such as linseeds, sesame, pumpkin and sunflower seeds which you can add to breads, rolls, stir-fries and salads. You can even grow your own sunflowers and then use the seeds – if you do this do not use any sprays.

● Invest in a large pack of oats to make porridge and add to muffins and crumbles and to thicken soups, casseroles and tagines.

● Buy skimmed milk and low-fat yogurt for cooking even if you are not keen on these in teas and coffees. Make rice puddings and custards with them to provide a low-calorie and low-GI comfort food.

● Choose rapeseed oil or olive oil in cooking and use a minimum of it. An oil-water spray may be useful to cut down on the amount of fat in cooking.

● Choose good-quality lean meat and a range of different types of fish and poultry.

● Invest in a wide range of herbs; the fresh ones are delicious and can be a basis for growing on at home. Also try a range of spices to flavour dishes.

Cooking

● The more highly processed the food then the higher the GI. Consider apples: a whole apple will have a lower GI than stewed apple or apple juice. The more breaking down that the body has to do to release the glucose from a food then the lower the GI. Try to keep foods as whole as possible, i.e. do not peel fruit and vegetables and try not to mash or purée them. If you are making soup, blend only half of it and enjoy the chunky textures.

● Try to use a minimum of spread on bread, and you may find that eating grain breads and rolls with their tasty, nutty flavour means that you do not need a spread at all.

● To reduce the calorie content of meals ensure that fat is trimmed from all meats and the skin is stripped from poultry before eating.

● Where a fat or oil is needed in cooking use an oil spray or even a pastry brush to spread oil over the bottom of a pan or over potatoes or vegetables for roasting.

● Stir-fries can actually be cooked in a little water rather than oil to start them off.

● Dry-fry pans, which have a special lid or a shiny surface on the inside of the lid, can be used to brown meat or chunks of vegetables. Using such a reflective surface on a lid can even be used to fry eggs successfully. Just use a spray of oil or a brush full of oil in the pan to start the process.

● To keep the fat level of dishes down make sure you bake, grill, steam, microwave, casserole or braise rather than deep-fat fry. Remember that batters and breadcrumbs really absorb a lot of fat so avoid these coatings on fish and chicken, or oven bake them if they do tempt you.

● Limit the amount of salt in cooking by using a range of herbs and spices.

Packed lunches

Many of us have to take packed lunches, so eating a lunch with a lower GI will help to keep us from feeling hungry all afternoon. The resulting more moderate and sustained level of blood glucose will also make us feel more alert.

Choose a bean or pasta salad, use grain breads and rolls for sandwiches, have lentil and bean soups and follow these with fresh fruits, oat muffins, low-fat yogurts, seed cakes, peanuts, teacakes or slices of fruit breads.

Snacks

A quick bite to eat can be really useful in curbing hunger pangs, particularly for children, teenagers, those with digestive problems and those involved in sport.

There are masses of high-fat and high-sugar snacks available and there is nothing wrong with these as an occasional treat.

However, to keep the GI levels down and thus promote a feeling of fullness, snacks such as unpeeled fresh fruit, peanuts, oatcakes, oat biscuits, seeded bread and buns are much better.

You will find recipes for muffins and fruit breads as well as seeded rolls in this book, which are all excellent as snacks.

Convenience foods

When days are a rush it is useful to choose a chilled or frozen ready meal – indeed it can be a way of experimenting with new flavours which may tempt you to cook them yourself at a later date.

But, this 'snip and ping' way of eating, where we snip open the packet and put it in the microwave to await the ping that tells us it is ready, can be unbalanced as many of the foods can be high in fat and salt but with little fruit and vegetable content.

They are also often not very satisfying and the serving sizes can be small, so the nutritional information on the package is deceptive as you may end up eating the meal designed for two on your own. Compare these with the size you would serve at home if preparing fresh cooked dishes. The next time you make your own lasagne, make a larger quantity so you can freeze the extra and create your own healthy ready meals.

However, served with extras such as some vegetables, new potatoes cooked in their skins, seeded breads or rolls or pasta convenience foods can become a satisfying and balanced meal and one with a low GI.

Fresh vegetables can be bought ready prepared and take little time to cook, but a standby of packets of frozen vegetables is also valuable. They can be cooked in a microwave or quickly in a pan.

Eating out

It does not matter where you eat out – whether a fast-food or a deluxe restaurant – the same principles apply as at home for reducing the GI level of meals.

● Choose grainy breads and rolls in preference to white or wholemeal; if the restaurant does not serve those perhaps asking will stimulate them to do so.

● Choose chunky vegetable or lentil soups rather than smooth creamy ones.

● For main courses select grilled meat, fish or poultry or a low-fat vegetarian dish. Choose those entrées to be served with beans or peas for greater satisfaction.

● Pasta dishes with a tomato-based sauce, and beans can be an excellent way of reducing the GI level of main courses.

● Indian meals with lentils, chickpeas and beans are all naturally low in GI but may be high in fat so ask for them to be cooked without fat.

● Select items on the menu with a lower calorie content, e.g. those without pastry, creamy sauces and which have not been fried, and accompany these with lots of vegetables. Ask for the vegetables to be served without any butter.

● Choose a fruit-based pudding or ice cream for dessert. If you decide on a higher calorie pudding opt for ice cream rather than cream to go with it.

● As the final tip for eating out: try to curb the amount of alcohol and thus keep the calorie level down by drinking lots of water.

Fast foods and takeaways

When you are rushing around or travelling it is often tempting to grab a burger or pizza for a quick snack. That quick snack, though, can often leave you looking for another meal so try to plan in advance what you will eat or choose carefully from the fast-food or takeaway menu.

● Choose a seeded bun with your burger and avoid the mayo to save calories.

● Choose pizzas topped with vegetables rather than pepperoni, extra cheese or ham.

● Pasta is ideal provided a tomato rather than a creamy sauce accompanies it.

● If the fish and chip shop tempts you, have half a portion of chips, avoid the batter on the fish and fill up with some extra peas.

● Indian food with its range of pulses is ideal; just ask for the dish to be made with less fat and avoid the obviously fried items such as onion bhajis, samosas and fried rice. Opt for plain boiled rice, ask for the poppadoms to be cooked in a microwave rather than deep-fried, have a side dish of dal to fill up on and avoid the kormas because of the coconut cream they contain.

● At the Chinese takeaway, avoid fried rice and items such as battered sweet and sour prawns and opt for dishes with noodles, plain rice and plenty of vegetables.

● Most restaurants now offer a range of salads and those containing beans and sweetcorn are particularly useful thanks to their low GI.

● Choose whole fruit or chunky fruits as sweets. Opt for low-fat ice cream and at least avoid the cream with ordinary sundaes.

menu planning

These wonderful recipes that Antony has created provide a delicious basis for meals. They are a brilliant blend of ingredients with a low GI as well as being low in calories. The recipes are also low in fat, salt and sugar, and include large portions of vegetables and fruit, thus reflecting the guidelines for healthy eating.

All the recipes are straightforward and easy to prepare and can be included in family eating. The use of different ingredients is inspirational and encourages the cook to try other recipes as well as developing their own variations.

Portion sizes

One of the marvellous things about the recipes is that they offer really substantial portions. Unlike most other diets, you will find each meal really satisfying and won't crave extra food and snacks.

About the nutritional calculations

The recipes have been calculated to show the calories per portion. They also show the amount of fat and saturated fat per portion in grams. The sodium content of recipes per portion is also shown.

All of the recipes have been calculated based on the smallest number of portions, for example if a recipe makes 4–6 portions, the nutritional breakdown has been calculated for 4 portions.

Where salt is included in the recipe, we have allowed for ¼ teaspoon (2g) per 4 portions.

The majority of the recipes have been created to provide under 300 calories per portion to help you lose weight at a sensible rate. Once you have achieved your target weight, there are a number of recipes that are between 300 and 500 calories per portion (indicated by a green semi-circle at the top of the recipe).

Serving suggestions

These are given with most of the recipes and are an integral part of the diet. Not only do they complement the dish, they will also reduce the GI of the meal, so do please take note of them. Of course, you can alter them to suit your tastes, but try to add vegetables, potatoes in their skins, brown rice, noodles, pasta or grainy bread to each meal.

Menu planners

These menu planners have been put together based on the recipes from the book. They give an idea of how to eat a satisfying and healthy diet which is also low in calories and can thus help weight loss or weight maintenance. The menus allow for extra fruit and vegetables as well as a scraping of butter or low-fat spreads on bread. However, with seeded bread, people often find they do not need this as the bread is so tasty. Also there is a daily allowance made for 500ml (18fl oz) of skimmed or semi-skimmed milk in teas or coffees.

Plenty of fluid is also recommended as is water and diluted juices. Even the odd glass of wine can be included.

Menu 1

Breakfast
Egg White Omelette
1 slice of South African Seed Bread

Mid-Morning
Apple

Lunch
2 slices of South African Seed Bread with
  Lentil Spread
Herbed Leaf Salad

Red Fruits

Mid-Afternoon
Pear

Dinner
Pan Fried Mullet with Olives and
  Tomatoes
New Potatoes
Green Beans

Rice Pudding

Snack
Scotch Pancakes and Honey

Plenty of fluids throughout the day

Menu 2

Breakfast
Porridge with Berries

Mid-Morning
Banana

Lunch
Leek and Pea Soup

Simple Roast Chicken
Baked Sweet Potatoes and Roasted
  Vegetables
Broccoli

Summer Pudding
Low Fat Fromage Frais

Mid-Afternoon
Carrot and Pineapple Cake

Dinner
Rocket, Chicory and Parmesan Salad
Barley and Goat's Cheese Soufflé Bake

Whole Poached Apricots

Snack
Soda Bread Roll
Carrot Cocktail

Plenty of fluids throughout the day

Menu 3

Breakfast
Caribbean Smoothie

Mid-Morning
Blueberry Muffin

Lunch
Smoked Salmon and Cottage Cheese
  Sandwich
2 plums

Mid-Afternoon
Plain Low-Fat Yogurt with Cherries

Dinner
Thai Fish Cakes with Cucumber Relish
Large Green Salad with Beans
Fresh Fruit Salad

Snack
1 slice of Orange and Almond Cake

Plenty of fluids throughout the day

breakfasts and baking

blueberry muffins

Blueberries are wonderfully versatile fruits. They are great eaten fresh or cooked in pies or muffins and if you have a surplus in season, freeze them quickly and they won't lose their valuable nutrients. Fresh blueberries are one of the best sources of vitamin C.

MAKES 9 SMALL MUFFINS

250g (9oz) wholegrain plain flour
2 teaspoons baking powder
25g (1oz) raw cane sugar
150ml (1/4 pint) skimmed milk
1 medium egg
2 tablespoons vegetable oil
200g (7oz) blueberries – fresh or frozen

1 Preheat the oven to 180°C/350°F/gas mark 4.

2 Line nine holes of a muffin tray with paper muffin cases.

3 Mix the flour, baking powder and sugar together in a large mixing bowl.

4 In a separate bowl, whisk the milk, egg and oil together. Make a well in the centre of the flour and quickly fold in the liquid then add the blueberries.

5 Divide the mixture between the muffin cases and bake for 25–30 minutes until risen and golden. You can test whether the muffins are cooked by lightly pressing one; if the top springs back, they are ready.

Per muffin: 141 kcal, 4g fat, 0.5g sat fat, 0.15g sodium, 23g carbohydrate

porridge with berries

There is no better way to start the day than with a hot bowl of porridge. This is a really low-GI breakfast, especially compared to breakfast cereals, and will keep you satisfied until lunch, so no need for croissants at coffee time.

SERVES 6

200g (7oz) medium oatmeal or porridge oats
Pinch of salt
1/2 teaspoon ground cinnamon
Low-fat natural yogurt, to serve
350g (12oz) berries of your choice, fresh or frozen (such as
   strawberries, blackberries, raspberries, blueberries)

1 Put 1.2 litres (2 pints) water on to boil in a large saucepan. When it comes to the boil slowly pour in the oats, stirring continuously. Reduce the heat to a level where the surface of the porridge faintly 'burps'. Stir in the salt and cinnamon.

2 Leave to cook until the porridge has reached the desired consistency – this will take about 15 minutes for a sloppy texture or 20 minutes for a firmer one.

3 Spoon the porridge into six bowls, place a good spoonful of yogurt on top then add a ladleful of berries.

Per portion: 162 kcal, 3g fat, 0.2g sat fat, 0.07g sodium, 29g carbohydrate

egg white omelette with asparagus and herbs

By using only the egg whites in this omelette, you remove almost all the fat content of the egg, as that is concentrated in the yolk. The easiest way to separate an egg is to crack it open and pour the white into a bowl, while catching the yolk in the shell. Serve with wholegrain toast and some warmed cherry tomatoes.

SERVES 1

Small knob of unsalted butter
3 egg whites (keep yolks for another use)
1 tablespoon finely chopped herbs such as chives, tarragon
   or chervil
Salt and ground black pepper
6 thin asparagus spears, cooked and cut into 2.5cm
   (1in) sections and kept warm
Wholegrain bread, toasted
Cherry tomatoes

1 Heat the knob of butter in a small non-stick omelette pan over a medium heat.

2 Whisk the egg whites with a fork and add the herbs, a pinch of salt and ground black pepper. Pour the egg white into the omelette pan and with a fork quickly pull the edges to the centre, so the omelette cooks evenly.

3 When cooked but still creamy, place the warm asparagus in the centre and leave on the heat for a second longer. Then fold the omelette in half, giving the pan a light tap to loosen the omelette. Slide out on to a warm plate.

Per portion: 154 kcal, 10g fat, 5.9g sat fat, 0.38g sodium, 3g carbohydrate

breakfast kitcheri

A kitcheri is a traditional Indian vegetarian dish that evolved into kedgeree, an Anglo-Indian favourite. This recipe is a fusion of both, combining the lentils in kitcheri with fish from kedgeree. The result is a low-GI dish that is perfect for brunch or supper.

SERVES 4

250g (9oz) kipper, smoked haddock or salmon fillet
300ml (1/2 pint) skimmed milk
1 bay leaf
1 small onion, chopped
10g (1/2oz) unsalted butter
1 tablespoon curry paste
175g (6oz) cooked brown basmati rice
400g (14oz) tin of lentils, drained and rinsed
2 hard-boiled eggs, chopped
2 tablespoons chopped parsley
Ground black pepper

1 Cook your chosen combination of fish in the milk with the bay leaf over a medium heat for 5–7 minutes, then set aside to allow to cool slightly.

2 Meanwhile, cook the onion slowly in the butter until soft but not browned, then add the curry paste and stir to combine.

3 Remove the fish from the milk, reserving the milk but discarding the bay leaf and any skin or bone from the fish.

4 Add the rice and lentils to the onion and heat through, then add the flaked fish, hard-boiled eggs and parsley and stir. Add enough of the reserved milk (about 150ml/1/4 pint) to make the mixture luscious and moist, then season to taste with black pepper and serve immediately.

Per portion: 418 kcal, 20g fat, 4.9g sat fat, 0.66g sodium, 36g carbohydrate

muesli mix

Muesli is one of the healthiest ways to start the day. Shop-bought versions may contain added sugar, so it is well worth taking the time to make your own. You can vary the choice of nuts, seeds and fruit – try adding linseeds, which is a good source of omega-3 fatty acids.

SERVES 10

250g (9oz) porridge oats
100g (3¹/₂oz) bran flakes
25g (1oz) wheatgerm
25g (1oz) sunflower seeds
50g (2oz) sultanas or raisins
50g (2oz) hazelnuts or brazils, roughly chopped
175g (6oz) dried fruits such as pears, figs, apricots, chopped

Combine all the ingredients and store in an airtight container.

Per portion: 236 kcal, 7g fat, 0.4g sat fat, 0.10g sodium, 38g carbohydrate

apple and hazelnut muesli

This will keep in the fridge for 2–3 days. Add extra fruit juice or yogurt as required to give a spoonable consistency. You can add extra berries or chopped fruit.

SERVES 3–4

110g (4oz) porridge oats
250g (9oz) very low-fat natural yogurt
150ml (¹/₄ pint) apple juice
2 pink-skinned apples, such as Pink Lady or Gala, cored and
    coarsely grated
25g (1oz) chopped toasted hazelnuts

Combine all the ingredients together until well mixed.

Per portion: 298 kcal, 9g fat, 0.8g sat fat, 0.09g sodium, 46g carboyhdrate

tropical fruit shake

This is a really thick shake and a great way to get kids to increase their fruit intake. You can use either fresh or frozen tropical fruit, varying the choice depending on season or tastes.

SERVES 2

110g (4oz) tropical fruit, chopped
1 medium-ripe banana
1 tablespoon liquid honey
150ml (1/4 pint) skimmed milk
150ml (1/4 pint) orange juice
4 tablespoons low-fat natural yogurt

Blend all the ingredients in a liquidiser goblet. If using fresh fruit or if the fruit has defrosted you may want to add 3–4 ice cubes.

Pour into tall glasses to serve.

Per portion: 200 kcal, 2g fat, 0.6g sat fat, 0.13g sodium, 41g carbohydrate

caribbean smoothie

Here's a rich, luxurious breakfast drink. The addition of the wheat bran increases the fibre content.

SERVES 4–6

3 bananas, peeled and chopped
425ml (3/4 pint) pineapple juice
300ml (1/2 pint) skimmed milk
2 tablespoons coconut cream
2 tablespoons wheat bran

Blend all the ingredients in a liquidiser goblet until smooth enough to drink. Add extra juice or milk as necessary to create the perfect consistency. Pour into tall glasses to serve.

Per portion: 193 kcal, 5g fat, 3.9g sat fat, 0.05g sodium, 35g carbohydrate

mountain bread

For a plain version, simply omit the garlic and spices.

SERVES 16 – MAKES 32 SLICES

450g (1lb) wholegrain flour
300g (10^1/$_2$oz) semolina
2 teaspoons salt
^{3}/$_4$ teaspoon cayenne pepper
1^1/$_4$ tablespoons garlic, crushed – approximately
   1 medium head
^{1}/$_2$ teaspoon chilli powder
^{1}/$_2$ teaspoon ground black pepper
^{1}/$_2$ teaspoon paprika
Vegetable oil, for greasing
2 egg yolks, beaten
50g (2oz) sunflower seeds
25g (1oz) poppy seeds

1 Preheat the oven to 220°C/425°F/gas mark 7.

2 Mix together all the dry ingredients and place in a food-processor with a dough hook fitted. With the machine running on a slow speed, gradually add 450ml (³/4 pint) warm water (from the kettle) until a dough forms. Let the machine run for 5–8 minutes to knead well.

3 Break the dough into eight pieces and either pass through a pasta machine or roll out to 3mm (¹/8in) thick strips. Cut each piece into four. Place the dough pieces on lightly oiled non-stick baking sheets and brush lightly with egg yolk then sprinkle liberally with the seeds. Bake for about 15 minutes or until golden, remove and leave to cool for 5 minutes then transfer to a wire rack. Store in an airtight container.

Per 2 slices: 190 kcal, 4g fat, 0.5g sat fat, 0.25g sodium, 38g carbohydrate

carrot cocktail

Give your immune system a boost with this revitalising drink (photographed bottom left). Carrots provide lots of beta-carotene, which acts as an antioxidant and is a substance the body can change into vitamin A. The ginger will help digestion and fight off colds.

SERVES 1–2

300ml (1/2 pint) organic carrot juice
1cm (1/2in) piece of fresh ginger, peeled
1 stick of celery, sliced lengthways

1 Put all the ingredients into a liquidiser goblet and whizz until smooth. Pour over some crushed ice and serve with a stick of celery in each glass.

2 Serve with mountain bread (see opposite page) or a wholegrain bread roll.

Per portion: 80 kcal, 0.4g fat, 0g sat fat, 0.18g sodium, 19g carbohydrate

wholegrain soda bread or rolls

If you use milk instead of yogurt or buttermilk in this recipe you will only need to use about 350ml (12fl oz).

MAKES 1 LOAF (8 WEDGES) OR 16 ROLLS

500g (18oz) wholegrain brown flour
1 teaspoon salt
1 1/2 teaspoons bicarbonate of soda
1 teaspoon caster sugar
About 425ml (3/4 pint) skimmed milk, low-fat natural yogurt or buttermilk

1 Preheat the oven to 230°C/450°F/gas mark 8.

2 Stir the dry ingredients together in a mixing bowl. Make a well in the centre and pour in 350ml (12fl oz) milk or 450ml (3/4 pint) yogurt or buttermilk.

3 Using one hand in a circular motion, mix in the flour to form a dough which is softish without being too wet or sticky – add more milk or flour if necessary. Turn the dough out on to a floured board. Knead just enough to tidy the dough into a neat ball.

4 For bread pat the dough into a round 4cm (1 1/2in) deep and cut a deep cross on the surface. Bake for 15 minutes on a floured baking tray then reduce the heat to 200°C/400°F/gas mark 6 for a further 25–30 minutes. For rolls, cut the dough into 16 pieces. Bake for about 20 minutes at the higher temperature.

5 To test whether it is cooked, tap the bottom of the bread and if it sounds hollow, it is ready.

Per wedge or 2 rolls: 108 kcal, 1g fat, 0.1g sat fat, 0.24g sodium, 22g carbohydrate

scotch pancakes

These thick pancakes are also known as drop scones. Serve with fresh fruit and a light drizzle of honey.

SERVES 4 – MAKES 12

50g (2oz) wholegrain flour
50g (2oz) plain flour
1/2 teaspoon cream of tartar
1/2 teaspoon bicarbonate of soda
1 teaspoon golden caster sugar
1 medium egg, preferably free-range
75–100ml (3–31/2fl oz) semi skimmed milk

1 Put the wholegrain flour in a bowl then sift in the rest of the dry ingredients. Make a well in the centre with a wooden spoon and add the egg. Break the yolk and pour in the milk, mixing quickly to a thick batter. Do not beat, as this develops the gluten in the flour and prevents the pancakes from rising.

2 Fry spoonfuls of the mixture in a lightly greased, hot skillet or heavy frying pan for 1–2 minutes on each side until risen and golden and springy to the touch. Serve warm.

Per portion: 120 kcal, 2g fat, 0.8g sat fat, 0.17g sodium, 20g carbohydrate

passion fruit curd

Extremely simple to make, this delicious fruit preserve is great with wholegrain toast or oat cakes. It also makes a terrific gift, so if you see passion fruit going cheap why not buy in bulk and make a big batch?

SERVES 10 – MAKES 300ML (½ PINT)

110g (4oz) caster sugar
60g (21/2oz) unsalted butter
2 eggs, beaten
6 passion fruit, pulp and seeds

1 Stir the caster sugar with the unsalted butter in a non-stick saucepan over a moderate heat until the sugar has dissolved.

2 Add the eggs and the passion fruit pulp and seeds, stirring continuously over the gentlest of heat for about 10 minutes until thickened. Do not allow to boil. If preferred, use a glass bowl over a saucepan of simmering water.

3 Pour into a sterilised jar and refrigerate for up to 2 months.

Per portion: 108 kcal, 6g fat, 3.5g sat fat, 0.02g sodium, 12g carbohydrate

orange and almond cake

This moist cake has a texture reminiscent of baked cheesecake. Keep in the fridge in an airtight container and eat within 3–4 days.

SERVES 12–16

2 large thin-skinned oranges
200g (7oz) golden caster sugar
200g (7oz) ground almonds
1/2 teaspoon baking powder
6 eggs
Juice of 1/2 lemon

1 Put the oranges in a pan and cover with cold water. Bring to the boil, reduce the heat, cover and simmer for 2 hours. Top up with water if necessary so that they are always covered. Remove from the water and leave to cool.

2 Preheat the oven to 180°C/350°F/gas mark 4. Grease and line a 23cm (9in) cake tin.

3 Cut the oranges into chunks and remove any pips. Put the oranges in a food-processor with all the remaining ingredients and blitz until well mixed. Transfer the mixture to the prepared tin and bake for 45–60 minutes until risen and firm to the touch. Cool, then transfer to a wire rack.

Per slice: 223 kcal, 13g fat, 1.7g sat fat, 0.06g sodium, 22g carbohydrate

south african seed bread

This bread has an extremely low GI as the tough outer coating of the seeds makes them harder to break down. The seeds are also excellent sources of omega-3 fatty acids and phytoestrogens. Quick to mix and only one rising required, this heavily seeded bread always has a fairly flat top.

MAKES 2 LOAVES – 18 SLICES EACH

650g (1lb 6oz) strong wholegrain flour
50g (2oz) wheat bran
2 sachets fast-action yeast (usually 6 or 7g)
50g (2oz) sunflower seeds
50g (2oz) sesame seeds
50g (2oz) pumpkin seeds
50g (2oz) linseeds
25g (1oz) muscovado sugar
1 teaspoon salt
2 tablespoons vegetable oil

1 Grease 2 x 900g (2lb) loaf tins. Mix the flour, wheat bran, yeast, seeds, sugar and salt in a large bowl. Add the oil and 600ml (1 pint) hand-hot water and mix to a soft dough.

2 Divide the mixture between the tins, cover with an oiled polythene bag and leave to rise in a warm place until the mixture reaches the top of the tins (this will take 30–60 minutes).

3 Meanwhile, preheat the oven to 200°C/400°F/gas mark 6 and bake the loaves in the centre of the oven for about 40 minutes until risen and firm to the touch. Once cooked the loaves will sound hollow when tapped on the base. Cool on wire racks.

Per slice: 100 kcal, 4g fat, 0.5g sat fat, 0.06g sodium, 13g carbohydrate

carrot and pineapple cake

This is a moist, luscious cake filled with carrots, nuts and spices – a real treat. It also freezes well.

SERVES 16

450g (1lb) wholemeal self-raising flour
2 teaspoons baking powder
1/2 tablespoon ground cinnamon
1/2 teaspoon ground nutmeg
1/2 teaspoon ground allspice
110g (4oz) dark muscovado sugar
125ml (4fl oz) light olive oil
2 eggs, lightly beaten
350g (12oz) carrot, grated
50g (2oz) walnut pieces
110g (4oz) raisins
25g (1oz) desiccated coconut
250g (9oz) crushed pineapple in natural juice
Golden icing sugar to dust (optional)

1 Preheat the oven to 180°C/350°F/gas mark 4. Grease and line the base of a 23cm (9in) spring-release tin with greaseproof paper.

2 Mix all the dry ingredients together in a large bowl. Add the remaining ingredients except the icing sugar and mix well until evenly combined.

3 Transfer the mixture to the prepared tin and level the surface. Bake in the centre of the oven for about 1 hour until risen and golden and a fine metal skewer comes out clean when inserted in the cake.

4 Cool in the tin for 15 minutes then transfer to a wire rack until completely cold. Dust with icing sugar before serving.

Per slice: 259 kcal, 13g fat, 2.5g sat fat, 0.08g sodium, 34g carbohydrate

fruited tea bread

Moist loaves packed full of dried fruit – a slice makes a perfect snack. You need to soak the sultanas and raisins in hot tea overnight.

MAKES 2 LOAVES – 16 SLICES PER LOAF

200g (7oz) sultanas
200g (7oz) raisins
425ml (³/4 pint) hot tea
350g (12oz) wholemeal plain flour
2 teaspoons ground mixed spice
2 teaspoons baking powder
50g (2oz) light muscovado sugar
175g (6oz) dates, chopped
110g (4oz) ready-to-eat dried apricots, chopped
25g (1oz) butter, melted
2 eggs, beaten

1 Soak the sultanas and raisins in the tea overnight.

2 Preheat the oven to 160°C/325°F/gas mark 3.

3 Grease 2 x 450g (1lb) loaf tins and line the bases with greaseproof paper.

4 Place all the dry ingredients in a large bowl and mix well. Add the soaked fruit with any extra liquid, and the remaining ingredients and mix well. Divide between the tins and level the surface.

5 Bake for 50–60 minutes until risen and firm to the touch. Cool in the tins then transfer to a wire rack until cold.

Per slice: 98 kcal, 1g fat, 0.6g sat fat, 0.05g sodium, 21g carbohydrate

finnish barley bread

This is an unusual bread – with a crisp outer crust and a dense moist centre – perfect for anyone trying to cut out wheat. Great with soup or cheese.

MAKES 1 FLAT LOAF – 16 SLICES

400g (14oz) pearl barley
500ml (18fl oz) buttermilk
Vegetable oil, for greasing
250g (9oz) barley flour, plus a little extra
1 teaspoon baking powder
1 teaspoon salt

1 Combine the pearl barley and buttermilk in a medium-sized bowl, cover and leave to soak overnight.

2 Preheat the oven to 180°C/350°F/gas mark 4.

3 Lightly oil and flour a 20–23cm (8–9in) cast-iron frying pan.

4 Add 250ml (9fl oz) water to the buttermilk and barley mixture, then transfer to the blender and blend until the barley is well pulverised (it will not become a smooth purée).

5 Return this batter to the bowl, add the barley flour, baking powder and salt and mix well. Spoon the batter into the frying pan. Bake in the centre of the oven for about 1 hour. Leave to cool on a wire rack before serving.

Per slice: 158 kcal, 1g fat, 0.2g sat fat, 0.17g sodium, 36g carbohydrate

dried fruit compôte

Another great way to begin your day with a good helping of fruit and nuts. This low-GI breakfast will prevent you feeling hungry during the morning.

SERVES 4

110g (4oz) small dried apricots
50g (2oz) dried cherries
50g (2oz) dried blueberries
50g (2oz) dried figs, halved
50g (2oz) dried pears, halved
50g (2oz) dried mango, cut into bite-sized pieces
$1/2$ cinnamon stick
2 cloves
$1/2$ vanilla pod, split
Finely grated zest of $1/2$ lemon
Pinch saffron stamens
10g ($1/2$oz) flaked almonds, toasted
10g ($1/2$oz) pine nuts
Few drops orange or rose water (optional)

1 Place all the ingredients down to and including the saffron in a non-reactive saucepan and just cover with cold water. Bring to the boil, reduce the heat and simmer for 15 minutes.

2 Allow to cool then add the remaining ingredients. Serve with cereal, wheatgerm or low-fat natural yogurt.

Per portion: 189 kcal, 5g fat, 0.4g sat fat, 0.03g sodium, 34g carbohydrate

soups

garlic soup with white beans

This is literally a heart-warming soup because while garlic has long been used as a protection against evil creatures, it has more recently been found to have medicinal qualities. Not only is it antibacterial, it will also boost your immune system and help prevent blood from clotting. Garlic is full of minerals and vitamins too. Serve with wholegrain bread.

SERVES 6

2 large heads garlic, cloves separated and finely sliced
2 onions, finely chopped
1 teaspoon soft thyme leaves
25g (1oz) unsalted butter
25g (1oz) cornflour
1.5 litres (2½ pints) chicken or vegetable stock
425g (15oz) tin of cannellini or haricot beans (tinned in water)
1 tablespoon red wine vinegar
Ground black pepper
Chopped parsley or chives, to serve

1 In a large heavy-based saucepan, cook the garlic, onions and thyme in the butter over a medium heat until softened, adding a little stock if necessary to prevent sticking – this should take about 7 minutes. Reduce the heat, stir in the cornflour and cook until lightly browned.

2 Add the stock gradually, stirring to avoid lumps. Increase the heat, bring to the boil and simmer for 30 minutes.

3 In small batches, pour the soup into a liquidiser and blend until smooth. Return to the heat.

4 Drain and rinse the beans and add to the soup with the vinegar. Warm through. Season with black pepper and serve immediately sprinkled with herbs.

Per portion: 121 kcal, 4g fat, 2.2g sat fat, 0.20g sodium, 17g carbohydrate

tuscan tomato and bread soup

A rich, rustic Italian soup, where the bread reduces the GI of the overall meal. This is actually a meal in itself, so serve as a main course rather than a starter.

SERVES 6

1 tablespoon olive oil
1 onion, finely chopped
2 garlic cloves, crushed
1kg (2¼lb) ripe tomatoes, peeled, de-seeded and chopped
400g (14oz) tin of chopped tomatoes
4 thick slices wholegrain bread, roughly broken
Bunch of basil
Ground black pepper

1 Heat the oil in a large saucepan. Add the onion and garlic and fry gently until the onion is soft but not brown.

2 Add the fresh tomatoes and cook for 1 minute. Add the tinned tomatoes, bread and basil, reserving a few basil leaves.

3 Simmer for 15 minutes stirring occasionally, adding up to 600ml (1 pint) water to give a 'sloppy' consistency. Just before serving, season with pepper and fold in the reserved basil leaves.

Per portion: 146 kcal, 4g fat, 0.6g sat fat, 0.22g sodium, 25g carbohydrate

fragrant asian carrot and lentil soup

I have given a classic vegetarian soup a bit of a spicy twist, adding ginger, coriander and curry powder. Blending only half the soup keeps the GI low and gives it texture.

SERVES 6–8

10g (1/2oz) unsalted butter
1 1/2 tablespoons grated fresh root ginger
1/2 teaspoon each ground allspice, cumin and chilli powder
1/2 teaspoon curry powder
1/2 teaspoon ground coriander
2 onions, finely chopped
1 parsnip, chopped
1 stick of celery, chopped
500g (18oz) carrots, sliced
175g (6oz) red lentils, washed
50g (2oz) brown basmati rice
1.8 litres (3 pints) vegetable stock
400ml (14fl oz) tin of reduced-fat coconut milk
2 tablespoons fresh lime juice
3 tablespoons chopped fresh coriander

1 Melt the butter in a heavy-based saucepan, add the ginger, allspice, cumin, chilli powder, curry powder and ground coriander. Cook over a medium heat for 3 minutes.

2 Add the vegetables, stir to combine and cook for a further 8 minutes. Add the lentils and rice and stir in, before adding the stock. Bring to the boil and simmer for 30 minutes or until the vegetables are tender and the lentils have started to break down.

3 Blend half the soup in a liquidiser or food-processor until smooth. Return to the rest of the mixture, and add the coconut milk, lime juice and coriander. Heat through but do not let it boil again – this is important. Serve immediately.

Per portion: 215 kcal, 3g fat, 1.6g sat fat, 0.31g sodium, 39g carbohydrate

borlotti bean and cabbage soup

Borlotti are Italian beans traditionally used in stews and soups. They have a lovely smooth, slightly sweet taste that will enrich this thick winter soup.

SERVES 6

2 tablespoons extra-virgin olive oil
1 onion, finely chopped
3 garlic cloves, finely chopped
2 bay leaves
1 teaspoon soft thyme leaves
1 chilli, de-seeded and finely diced
4 tablespoons roughly chopped flat-leaf parsley
1 tablespoon chopped marjoram
1 x 400g (14oz) tin of chopped tomatoes
2 x 400g (14oz) tins of borlotti beans (tinned in water), drained and rinsed
700ml (1 1/4 pints) vegetable stock
450g (1lb) shredded greens (savoy, cavolo nero, spring greens)
Ground black pepper
Freshly grated parmesan (optional)

1 Heat the olive oil in a large saucepan over a medium heat, add the onion, garlic, bay leaves, thyme and chilli. Cook for about 10 minutes or until the onion has softened but still colourless.

2 Add the herbs and tomatoes and cook for 3 minutes. Add the beans, stock and 600ml (1 pint) of water and cook for 30 minutes at a steady simmer.

3 Add the shredded greens and cook for 10 minutes. Thin as required with extra water. Season to taste with black pepper. Pour into bowls and sprinkle with grated parmesan, if wished.

Per portion: 163 kcal, 5g fat, 0.7g sat fat, 0.45g sodium, 21g carbohydrate

health in a bowl

The title says it all. I have chucked in every healthy ingredient I can think of and waved my magic spoon.

SERVES 8

450g (1lb) thick-cut ham on the bone, chopped
2.4 litres (4 pints) chicken stock
4 tablespoons pearl barley
2 tablespoons Puy lentils
2 medium onions, sliced
4–6 medium carrots, diced
2 medium parsnips, diced
1/2 medium swede, diced
Ground black pepper
2 sprigs of thyme
2 bay leaves
Sprig of parsley
450g (1lb) potatoes in their skins, diced
1 small cabbage, chopped
1 leek, chopped
4 tablespoons chopped parsley
400g (14oz) tin of red kidney beans, drained and rinsed
4 tablespoons snipped chives

1 Place the ham in a saucepan and cover with stock. Bring to the boil, skim any scum, then add the pearl barley and lentils.

2 Bring to the boil, reduce the heat and simmer for 15 minutes. Add the onions, carrots, parsnips, swede, pepper, thyme, bay leaves and parsley. Bring to the boil, reduce the heat and simmer gently for a further 15 minutes.

3 Add the potatoes and cabbage and return to the boil. Simmer until they are just tender (about 15 minutes).

4 Add the chopped leek and parsley and cook for a further 5 minutes or until the leek is just tender.

5 Add the beans and warm through. Ladle into soup bowls and serve sprinkled with chives.

Per portion: 264 kcal, 3g fat, 0.8g sat fat, 0.97g sodium, 42g carbohydrate

tomato, pasta and flageolet bean soup

The flageolet is the prince of beans, picked when young and tender. Combined with pasta and wholegrain bread, the GI of this soup is extremely low.

SERVES 4

10g (1/2oz) unsalted butter
1 onion, finely diced
2 garlic cloves, finely diced
Large pinch of dried chilli flakes
400g (14oz) tin of chopped tomatoes with basil
1 litre (13/4 pints) vegetable stock
75g (3oz) small pasta shapes
1 sachet bouquet garni
375g (13oz) tin of flageolet beans (tinned in water), drained and rinsed
Ground black pepper
2 tablespoons pesto (optional)

1 Melt the butter in a saucepan, then fry the onion, garlic and chilli flakes until soft but still colourless, adding a dash of water if necessary to prevent sticking. Add the tomatoes, stock, pasta and bouquet garni, and simmer for 15 minutes. Stir in the beans, bring back to a simmer and season to taste with black pepper. Add extra stock to thin as necessary.

2 Serve in warm soup bowls, with a little pesto, if wished, and some hot crusty wholegrain bread.

Per portion: 176 kcal, 4g fat, 2g sat fat, 0.54g sodium, 27g carbohydrate

leek and pea soup

Peas lower the GI of a dish, but it doesn't matter if you can't find fresh ones – nowadays frozen peas are just as nutritious. Serve with some wholegrain croûtons.

SERVES 4–6

10g (1/2oz) unsalted butter
2 leeks, chopped, washed and well drained
1 teaspoon soft thyme leaves
1 garlic clove, finely chopped
900ml (11/2 pints) chicken or vegetable stock
275g (10oz) shelled or frozen peas
1 round lettuce, washed and chopped
1 tablespoon finely chopped mint
Ground black pepper

1 Melt the butter in a saucepan and cook the leeks with the thyme and garlic over a gentle heat until soft but not brown, adding a dash of water if necessary to prevent sticking.

2 Add the stock and bring to the boil. Add the peas and lettuce and continue cooking until the peas are tender.

3 Stir in the mint and, if you like, liquidise about half the mixture. Return to the rest of the soup, reheat and season to taste with black pepper.

Per portion: 101 kcal, 5g fat, 2.1g sat fat, 0.29g sodium, 10g carbohydrate

barley and bean soup

Pearl barley is literally the pearl of the barley as the outer layers, including the bran, have been stripped off and it is then polished until smooth. Even though most of the fibre has been removed, it is still nutritious and a common ingredient in soups.

SERVES 4–6

2 tablespoons olive oil
1 large onion, chopped
2 garlic cloves, chopped
150g (5oz) pearl barley or barley
1 teaspoon soft thyme leaves
1 bay leaf
1.2 litres (2 pints) chicken stock
425g (15oz) tin of black-eyed beans or kidney beans (tinned in water), drained and rinsed
Ground black pepper
2 tablespoons chopped mint
2 tablespoons chopped coriander
1 tablespoon chopped chives

1 Heat the oil in a saucepan and cook the onion and garlic gently until soft but still colourless – this should take about 10 minutes. Add the barley, thyme and bay leaf, stir to combine. Add the chicken stock and heat to boiling, reduce the heat and simmer for about 1 hour. Add the beans for the last 10 minutes.

2 Liquidise half the soup (if wished) then return to the rest of the soup and season with black pepper. Add extra stock to thin as necessary. Just before serving stir in the herbs.

Per portion: 274 kcal, 7g fat, 1.0g sat fat, 0.52g sodium, 48g carbohydrate

celtic lamb and barley soup

SERVES 8

110g (4oz) pearl barley or brown wholegrain barley
3 lamb shanks
2 carrots, sliced
2 celery stalks, sliced
1 onion, chopped
2 leeks, shredded and washed
2 bay leaves
2 parsnips, sliced
2 turnips, diced
Heart of a small cabbage, shredded
2 potatoes with skins, diced
Ground black pepper
2 tablespoons chopped parsley

1 Cover the barley with cold water, bring to the boil and strain. Trim the lamb of excess fat and place in a saucepan with 3 litres (5¼ pints) water, the barley, carrots, celery, onions, leeks and bay leaves. Bring to the boil, skim, reduce the heat and simmer for 2 hours.

2 Leave to cool overnight, and remove any fat that forms. Remove the meat and shred into small pieces. Return the meat to the stock and add the remaining vegetables.

3 Cook for a further 15 minutes until the vegetables are tender, topping up with more stock as necessary. Season with pepper and serve sprinkled with chopped parsley.

Per portion: 246 kcal, 8g fat, 3.5g sat fat, 0.06g sodium, 29g carbohydrate

pumpkin and white bean soup

You will never run out of uses for pumpkin. Roast it, mash it or put it in a pie or soup, and while it is cooking, carve a ghoulish face in the shell.

SERVES 6

1 small pumpkin, peeled, de-seeded and diced
2 leeks, white part only, finely sliced
1 carrot, finely diced
2 sticks of celery, finely diced
2 garlic cloves, finely diced
12 sage leaves, shredded
1 tablespoon olive oil
1.2 litres (2 pints) chicken or vegetable stock
2 bay leaves
400g (14oz) tin of cannellini beans (tinned in water), drained and rinsed
2 tablespoons chopped parsley
Ground black pepper
Grated parmesan, to serve (optional)

1 Fry the vegetables, garlic and sage in the olive oil, and cook for approximately 7 minutes, adding a dash of water to prevent sticking.

2 Pour in the stock and bay leaves and bring to the boil. Reduce the heat and simmer for 15–20 minutes. Add the beans, heat through then stir in the parsley. Season with black pepper to taste.

3 Serve as a chunky soup (or if preferred, purée half and return to the rest of the soup). Sprinkle with parmesan, if desired, and eat with wholegrain bread.

Per portion: 124 kcal, 4g fat, 0.6g sat fat, 0.20g sodium, 16g carbohydrate

chicken, chilli and corn soup

This is a classic Mexican recipe and a really comforting dish. If you like, you can thicken the stock by mixing 1–2 teaspoons of cornflour with a little of the stock before adding the rest.

SERVES 4–6

1 teaspoon unsalted butter
4 jalapeño (medium-strength) chillies, de-seeded and finely diced
2 slices back bacon, diced
1 onion, finely diced
1 garlic clove, finely diced
1 teaspoon soft thyme leaves
1 large sweet potato, peeled and diced
2 skinless chicken breast fillets, diced
250g (9oz) fresh, frozen or tinned corn kernels
1.2 litres (2 pints) chicken stock
Ground black pepper

1 Melt the butter in a non-stick saucepan and fry the chillies, bacon, onion and garlic until the onion is soft, adding a dash of water if necessary to prevent sticking.

2 Add the remaining ingredients and simmer, covered, for 20 minutes. Season to taste with black pepper.

Per portion: 141 kcal, 3g fat, 1.2g sat fat, 0.57g sodium, 11g carbohydrate

tabbouleh

A classic Middle Eastern salad, this makes a perfect appetiser or accompaniment to the kofta meatballs on page 134. Or make a mezze with falafel (page 82), either of the aubergine recipes on pages 84–85, together with radishes, lettuce leaves and wholemeal flatbread and finish off with mint tea.

SERVES 4

175g (6oz) cracked wheat
Salt and ground black pepper
Juice of 2 small lemons
2 tablespoons extra-virgin olive oil
75g (3oz) flat-leaf parsley, chopped
25g (1oz) mint leaves, chopped
Bunch of spring onions, finely sliced
3 plum tomatoes, quartered

1 Soak the cracked wheat in cold water for 20 minutes, drain and squeeze dry. Put the wheat in a glass bowl and season with salt and black pepper, add the lemon juice and the olive oil. Allow to rest for 30 minutes.

2 Add the parsley, mint and spring onions. Check the seasoning and top the salad with the plum tomatoes.

Per portion: 227 kcal, 7g fat, 0.9g sat fat, 0.21g sodium, 37g carbohydrate

herbed leaf salad

There are two ways of seasoning a salad. You can either season the dressing or the salad itself, but this can lead to trouble because if you season the leaves themselves and the leaves are damp, you're likely to end up with a mouthful of salt. The way round this is to season around the inside of the bowl (before dressing the salad) and toss the leaves in the bowl. In theory they will then be evenly seasoned.

SERVES 4–6

1 garlic clove, peeled
4 tablespoons mixed fresh soft herbs, washed and dried
*   (chervil, tarragon, dill, basil, marjoram, flat-leaf parsley,*
*   mint, chives or sorrel)*
350g (12oz) mixed salad leaves, washed, dried and torn
*   (curly endive, baby spinach, rocket, radicchio, chicory,*
*   watercress, trevise, oak leaf, dandelion, nasturtium)*
Salt and ground black pepper
4–6 tablespoons reduced-calorie salad dressing

1 Rub a wooden salad bowl with the raw garlic. Combine the herbs and the salad leaves and mix thoroughly. Season (see above).

2 Dress the leaves, but don't drown them. Serve immediately – once dressed, try not to let the salad sit around for too long or the leaves will go soggy. If you like, scatter over some wholegrain croûtons or flakes of parmesan or pecorino.

Per portion: 36 kcal, 1.1g fat, 0.1g sat fat, 0.32g sodium, 5g carbohydrate

salad of asparagus with avocado and walnuts

This is a fusion of Western ingredients with an Eastern dressing. Try to find locally grown asparagus as it will be much more tender and delicious than imported varieties. In England, the asparagus season starts in May, so buy some as soon as it appears in the shops.

SERVES 4

24 asparagus spears, trimmed
1 ripe Hass avocado, stone removed, peeled and sliced
2 tablespoons lemon juice
2 heads chicory (Belgian endive)
100g (3¹/₂oz) lamb's lettuce (mâche) or watercress, washed
2 tablespoons walnut pieces
2 tablespoons snipped chives

Dressing
2 tablespoons light soy sauce
¹/₂ tablespoon grated ginger
1 garlic clove, crushed
1 tablespoon olive oil
Ground black pepper

1 Cook the asparagus in fast-boiling water for about 5 minutes until just tender, drain and refresh in iced water, drain again and set aside.

2 Toss the avocado with half the lemon juice.

3 For the dressing, combine the soy, ginger, garlic, remaining lemon juice and oil, then season with pepper.

4 Arrange the salad leaves on each of four plates, arrange the asparagus spears on top of the leaves and drizzle with dressing. Scatter with the walnuts, avocado and chives.

Per portion without dressing: 141 kcal, 11g fat, 1.9g sat fat, 0.01g sodium, 5g carbohydrate

Per portion with dressing: 172 kcal, 13g fat, 2.3g sat fat, 0.01g sodium, 6g carbohydrate

panzanella

An Italian bread salad, this is one instance where the bread shouldn't be fresh. The base ingredients are bread, tomatoes and onion, and a handful of basil with a drop or two of olive oil are always welcome.

SERVES 4

2 thick slices day-old wholegrain bread
6 ripe tomatoes, cubed
1 small red onion, finely diced
¹/₂ cucumber, diced
1 stick of celery, finely sliced
2 garlic cloves, crushed
Small handful of basil leaves, torn into small pieces
2 tablespoons olive oil
1 tablespoon red wine vinegar
Ground black pepper

1 Cut or tear the bread into small pieces.

2 Place the pieces in a bowl and sprinkle with a little cold water – the bread should be moist but not soggy.

3 Add the tomatoes, onion, cucumber, celery, garlic and basil and mix gently.

4 Mix together the oil and vinegar and season with black pepper. Shake well to make a dressing and pour over the salad.

5 Toss the salad well, and leave it for 30 minutes before serving to allow the flavours to develop.

Per portion: 142 kcal, 7g fat, 1.1g sat fat, 0.17g sodium, 17g carbohydrate

salad of mushrooms, jumbo prawns & spinach

SERVES 4

250g (9oz) button mushrooms, wiped and sliced
175g (6oz) cooked jumbo prawns, peeled and halved
150g (5oz) baby spinach (or other light salad leaves), washed
  and dried
2 tablespoons rice vinegar
2 tablespoons lemon juice
1 tablespoon light soy sauce
2 tablespoons vegetable oil
3 spring onions, sliced

1 Combine together the mushrooms, prawns and spinach.

2 In a separate bowl mix the rice vinegar, lemon juice, soy
sauce and vegetable oil. Pour this dressing over the salad,
toss well and sprinkle with the spring onions.

Per portion: 124 kcal, 7g fat, 0.9g sat fat, 1.74g sodium,
2g carbohydrate

warm broccoli salad

SERVES 2

1 small onion, grated
4 anchovy fillets, mashed
2 teaspoons capers, rinsed and chopped
Juice of 1/2 small lemon
1 tablespoon extra-virgin olive oil
1 tablespoon chopped mint
275g (10oz) small broccoli florets
Ground black pepper

Thoroughly mix the onion, anchovies, capers, lemon juice,
olive oil and mint in a bowl. Steam the broccoli for 3–5
minutes, then drain and toss with the rest of the salad.
Season with black pepper and serve immediately. This salad is
also good served at room temperature and is delicious tossed
with wholewheat pasta.

Per portion: 166 kcal, 11g fat, 1.1g sat fat,
0.80g sodium, 6g carbohydrate

duck salad with chunky mango salsa

SERVES 4

2 duck breast fillets, skin on
200g (7oz) assorted salad leaves
110g (4oz) mangetout, shredded, or fine green beans,
  cooked

Salsa
1 mango, diced
Small bunch of mint, chopped
Small bunch of coriander, chopped
Juice of 1 lime
1 red onion, diced
1 chilli, de-seeded and finely chopped
3 tomatoes, diced
Salt and ground black pepper

1 Preheat the oven to 190°C/375°F/gas mark 5.

2 Score criss-crosses close together on the skin of the duck;
so that most of the fat is released when cooking.

3 Place the duck, skin side down, in an ovenproof frying pan
over a medium heat and cook for 4–5 minutes. Turn the
duck over and cook for 1–2 minutes then transfer to the oven
and cook for 5–10 minutes depending on how pink you like it.

4 Meanwhile combine the ingredients for the salsa and season.
When the duck is cooked it will feel slightly springy to the
touch (if pink) or firm (well done). Remove from the oven
and leave to rest for 5–10 minutes, then slice. Arrange on
the salad leaves with the mangetout and serve with the salsa.

Per portion: 151 kcal, 5g fat, 1.4g sat fat, 0.28g sodium,
13g carbohydrate

tuna and bean salad

An all–time favourite Italian salad, this won't take long to make and is great for lunch.

SERVES 2

400g (14oz) tin of cannellini beans, drained and rinsed
1 small red onion, halved and finely sliced
200g (7oz) tin of tuna in oil
2 tablespoons roughly chopped flat-leaf parsley
Lemon juice or wine vinegar, to taste
Ground black pepper

Mix all the ingredients together and serve.

Per portion: 328 kcal, 10g fat, 1.6g sat fat, 0.28g sodium, 23g carbohydrate

sardine and potato salad

SERVES 2

250g (9oz) waxy new potatoes in their skins
125g (4¹/₂oz) tin of sardines in oil
1 tablespoon lemon juice or wine vinegar, or to taste
1 teaspoon Dijon mustard
Ground black pepper
2 large handfuls of salad leaves
3 spring onions, finely sliced

1 Steam the potatoes until tender then slice. While the potatoes are cooking whisk together the oil from the sardines, lemon juice and mustard and season with pepper. Thin with a little potato water if liked.

2 Mix the potatoes with the dressing and pile on to the salad. Top with the sardines and sprinkle with the spring onions and more pepper.

Per portion: 231 kcal, 9g fat, 1.9g sat fat, 0.35g sodium, 22g carbohydrate

warm calf's liver salad

Calf's liver has a soft texture and gentle flavour and is my favourite kind of liver. Although it has fallen out of fashion, liver is a good source of iron, zinc, vitamins A and B12 and protein, but try to buy organic meat.

SERVES 4

175g (6oz) baby spinach leaves
10g (¹/₂oz) unsalted butter
1 tablespoon olive oil
4 shallots, cut in quarters
1 teaspoon soft thyme leaves
2 slices back bacon, cut in strips
350g (12oz) calf's, lamb's or chicken livers
24 button mushrooms, quartered
Ground black pepper
2 tablespoons pine nuts
2 tablespoons balsamic vinegar

1 Wash and dry the baby spinach leaves and arrange on four plates.

2 Heat the butter and olive oil in a large non-stick frying pan and fry the shallots until brown and softening. Add the thyme, bacon and liver and increase the heat. Cook the liver until brown on all sides but still pink in the middle.

3 Remove liver, shallots and bacon and keep warm. Add the mushrooms to the pan and toss together, then season with black pepper. With a slotted spoon place an equal amount on each plate.

4 Add the pine nuts to the pan, and cook until golden. Deglaze the pan with the vinegar and spoon a little of the warm dressing over each salad.

Per portion: 222 kcal, 14g fat, 3.9g sat fat, 0.33g sodium, 2g carbohydrate

starters, sandwiches and snacks

falafel

A Middle Eastern speciality, falafel are sometimes made with dried broad beans instead of chickpeas, especially in Egypt. A good falafel is light, fragrant and fluffy with a crisp shell. It is also traditionally deep fried, but this is a much healthier version.

SERVES 4–6 – MAKES 24

250g (9oz) dried chickpeas, soaked overnight then
    well drained
1 garlic clove
Handful of parsley
Handful of coriander
2 tablespoons chopped mint
$1/2$ onion, roughly chopped
$1/4$ teaspoon cayenne pepper
$1/2$ teaspoon ground cumin
$1/2$ teaspoon ground black pepper
$1/2$ teaspoon baking powder
$1/2$ teaspoon ground coriander
Vegetable oil for frying
Low-fat natural yogurt, or wholemeal pitta, shredded salad
    and pickled chillies to serve (optional)

1 Blend all the ingredients in a food-processor to form a manageable mixture.

2 Shape into 24 small patties and fry in a thin film of oil in a non-stick frying pan until golden brown on both sides. Serve as a snack with natural yogurt – or for a more substantial meal, in pitta bread pockets with shredded salad and pickled chillies.

Per portion: 135 kcal, 7g fat, 0.7g sat fat, 0.06g sodium, 13g carbohydrate

piquant avocado salsa

Avocados are full of heart-protective monounsaturates. Their sweet, creamy flavour is tempered here by the herbs and spices to make a great starter or party food.

SERVES 2

1 ripe avocado, peeled and stoned
1 tomato, de-seeded and diced
2 spring onions, sliced
Juice of $1/2$–1 lime
1 chilli, de-seeded and finely chopped
Pinch of ground cumin
Pinch of ground coriander
2 tablespoons finely chopped coriander
1 teaspoon chilli oil
Salt and ground black pepper

1 Mash the avocado with the back of a fork, but do not make it too smooth. Fold in all the other ingredients and season to taste.

2 Serve with crostini or corn chips.

Per portion: 163 kcal, 16g fat, 3.2g sat fat, 0.21g sodium, 3g carbohydrate

lentil spread

Like tapenade, this Mediterranean paste is made with olives and capers and will keep for 2–3 days if stored in an airtight container and refrigerated. Serve with crostini or bruschetta.

SERVES 6

250g (9oz) Puy or continental lentils, rinsed
300ml (1/2 pint) vegetable stock
2 tablespoons chopped garlic
2 tablespoons chopped sun-dried tomatoes
1 tablespoon chopped sun-dried peppers
2 tablespoons capers
3 anchovy fillets
3 tablespoons chopped black or green olives
1 tablespoon extra-virgin olive oil
2 tablespoons lemon juice
4 tablespoons chopped parsley

1 Cook the lentils in the stock with the garlic, tomatoes and peppers until just tender – about 20 minutes – adding a little extra stock if necessary to prevent sticking.

2 Put the contents of the pan in a food-processor and whizz briefly with the rest of the ingredients to make a coarse spread. Add extra stock to soften the mixture as required.

Per portion: 187 kcal, 6g fat, 0.6g sat fat, 0.55g sodium, 24g carbohydrate

aubergine 'caviar'

This is a feisty dip with loads of flavour. Aubergines are a good source of fibre and potassium, while the onion, garlic and ginger will boost your immune system.

SERVES 6

3 large aubergines
1 tablespoon sesame oil
1 small red onion, finely diced
2 garlic cloves, finely diced
1 large knob of ginger, peeled and grated
1 red chilli, de-seeded and finely diced
1 red pepper, roasted or grilled, peeled, de-seeded and diced
2–4 spring onions, finely sliced
2 tablespoons finely chopped coriander

1 Preheat the oven to 190°C/375°F/gas mark 5. Prick the aubergines all over with a fork and bake on a tray for 45–60 minutes or until they feel very soft. Keep warm.

2 Meanwhile heat the sesame oil in a small frying pan and cook the red onion, garlic, ginger and chilli until soft but not brown.

3 Cut the aubergines in half lengthways and scoop out the flesh (squeezing out the excess liquid) into a food-processor then add the cooked onion mixture. Whizz briefly. Fold in the other ingredients. Alternatively, chop the aubergine pulp and stir in the rest of the ingredients.

5 Serve at room temperature with wholegrain toast.

Per portion: 81 kcal, 4g fat, 0.7g sat fat, 0.01g sodium, 10g carbohydrate

chunky aubergine and yogurt dip

Aubergines used to be sliced and covered in salt before cooking to get rid of any bitterness. This is no longer necessary because of revised growing techniques, but it will reduce the amount of oil the aubergine soaks up.

SERVES 4

500g (18oz) aubergines, cut in 5cm (2in) cubes
1 tablespoon extra-virgin olive oil
500g (18oz) plum tomatoes, peeled, de-seeded and cubed
175ml (6fl oz) tomato juice
2 green chillies, finely diced
1 tablespoon chopped garlic
2 tablespoons white wine vinegar
Salt and ground black pepper
175ml (6fl oz) 0% fat Greek-style natural yogurt
4 spring onions, finely sliced
2 tablespoons chopped parsley

1 Place the aubergine in a flameproof baking dish with the olive oil, tomatoes, tomato juice and chillies. Cook over a medium heat for 20 minutes.

2 Stir in the garlic and vinegar and continue to cook for a further 20 minutes, adding a little extra tomato juice if necessary until the aubergine is very tender. Season. Remove from the heat, then stir in the yogurt and sprinkle with the spring onions and parsley.

3 Serve warm or at room temperature with wholemeal pitta bread or as a vegetable accompaniment.

Per portion: 101 kcal, 4g fat, 0.9g sat fat, 0.35g sodium, 12g carbohydrate

spicy mushrooms on toast

SERVES 2

1 onion, finely diced
1 teaspoon grated ginger
1 garlic clove, finely diced
1 chilli, de-seeded and finely diced
1 tablespoon sesame oil
275g (10oz) button mushrooms, quartered
150ml (1/4 pint) dry white wine
1 tablespoon light soy sauce
Ground black pepper
2 large slices wholegrain bread, toasted
2 spring onions, sliced
1 tablespoon chopped coriander
1 tablespoon chopped mint
2 tablespoons 0% fat Greek-style natural yogurt

1 Cook the onion, ginger, garlic and chilli in the oil over a moderate heat until the onion is softened. Turn up the heat, add the mushrooms and cook for 5 minutes.

2 Add the wine and soy sauce and cook for 5 minutes or until the mushrooms are cooked and the liquid has reduced to about 4 tablespoons. Season to taste with black pepper.

3 With a slotted spoon lift the mushrooms and place them on the toast, scatter with the spring onions, coriander and mint, and top with a spoonful of yogurt.

Per portion: 296 kcal, 8g fat, 1.3g sat fat, 0.64g sodium, 33g carbohydrate

mediterranean carrot mezza

This is a gorgeous mix of carrots, fruit, nuts and spices. Make them in advance and take them as a packed lunch.

SERVES 4 – MAKES 24

10 medium carrots
2 slices wholegrain bread, rubbed into crumbs
12 dried apricots, finely diced
1 tablespoon sultanas, chopped
4 spring onions, finely diced
3 tablespoons pine nuts
1 teaspoon chilli flakes
2 teaspoons finely grated orange zest
1 egg
6 tablespoons mixed chopped mint and dill
Salt and ground black pepper
Sunflower oil for frying

To serve
Low-fat natural yogurt
Chopped red onion
Coriander leaves, shredded

1 Steam and roughly mash half the carrots, and grate the rest. Combine them together then add the remaining ingredients up to the seasoning and knead well. If the mixture is too wet add more breadcrumbs – it should be soft and slightly damp.

2 Mould the mixture into 24 small 'cakes' then 'dry' fry in a non-stick pan sprayed with oil until brown on both sides.

3 Serve with low-fat natural yogurt, generously flavoured with red onion and coriander.

Per portion: 264 kcal, 10g fat, 1.2g sat fat, 0.39g sodium, 40g carbohydrate

broad bean and rosemary mash

Great as a vegetable with grilled meats or fish, you could also serve this as a dip with bruschetta or wholemeal pitta bread. If you prefer, you could choose other beans or peas.

SERVES 6

1 tablespoon extra-virgin olive oil
2 garlic cloves, crushed
1 tablespoon very finely chopped rosemary (if using peas, use 1–2 tablespoons mint)
1 small onion, finely chopped
450g (1lb) cooked broad beans, with some cooking liquor
Juice of 1/2 lemon
Ground black pepper

1 Pour the olive oil into a saucepan then add the garlic, rosemary and onion and cook over a medium heat until the onion is soft but still colourless.

2 Add the beans, lemon juice and a generous grinding of pepper and cook gently for 10 minutes. Remove from the heat and roughly mash or whizz in a food-processor. Add some bean cooking liquor if the mixture is too dry.

Per portion: 87 kcal, 4g fat, 0.5g sat fat, 0.02g sodium, 8g carbohydrate

american prawn cocktail

The American version is very different from a British prawn cocktail. They use large cooked 'shrimp' and serve it with a hot red cocktail sauce whereas in Britain, small prawns are drowned in mayonnaise, mixed with Worcestershire sauce and tomato ketchup, then sprinkled with paprika.

SERVES 6

450g (1lb) cooked jumbo prawns (about 30), shelled and de-veined
4 little gem lettuce, quartered
Lemon wedges, to serve

Sauce
75ml (3fl oz) chilli sauce
75ml (3fl oz) reduced sugar and salt tomato ketchup
1/2 tablespoon fresh lemon juice
1 tablespoon grated horseradish (not creamed)
Dash of Worcestershire sauce
1/2 stick of celery, very finely diced
Dash of Tabasco sauce

1 Combine all the sauce ingredients and keep in the fridge until needed.

2 Arrange the prawns on a platter with the lettuce and lemon wedges. Serve the cocktail sauce separately.

Per portion: 99 kcal, 1g fat, 0.1g sat fat, 0.36g sodium, 8g carbohydrate

kipper pâté

A kippered herring is quintessentially British, but the French have claimed that the kipper was first made in the north of France. Either way, I have transformed it into a low-fat pâté that is perfect for a light lunch.

SERVES 4

3 cooked kipper fillets, skinned
75g (3oz) low-fat soft cheese or cottage cheese
6 tablespoons low-fat natural yogurt
Lemon juice, to taste
Pinch of chilli powder
1/2 teaspoon freshly ground black pepper
Pinch of nutmeg

1 Put the kippers in a food-processor with the cheese, yogurt, lemon juice, chilli powder, pepper and nutmeg. Blend until fairly smooth. Season to taste. Transfer to a bowl, cover and refrigerate overnight.

2 Serve the pâté with hot wholegrain toast and cucumber sticks or cherry tomatoes if wished.

Per portion: 176 kcal, 11g fat, 2.1g sat fat, 0.59g sodium, 5g carbohdrate

purple figs with parma ham and minted yogurt

SERVES 4

8 large ripe purple figs
200g (7oz) thinly sliced Parma ham

Minted yogurt
2 tablespoons finely diced cucumber
150ml (1/4 pint) low-fat natural yogurt
1 tablespoon chopped mint
Ground black pepper

1 To make the yogurt, combine all the ingredients and season to taste with black pepper.

2 Slice the figs vertically in 4 and arrange on plates with the ham. Serve the yogurt separately.

Per portion: 363 kcal, 8g fat, 2.3 sat fat, 1.09g sodium, 56g carbohydrate

spiced chicken pitta sandwich

More of a meal than a snack, this is reminiscent of the Greek souvlaki, aromatic pitta bread stuffed with spiced lamb and yogurt.

SERVES 4

2 onions, thinly sliced
2 garlic cloves
1/2 teaspoon ground cinnamon
1 teaspoon ground cumin
1 teaspoon ground coriander
2 teaspoons ground paprika
1/2 teaspoon chilli powder
4 tablespoons chopped coriander
2 tablespoons chopped mint
350g (12oz) chicken stir-fry pieces
1 tablespoon olive oil
4 wholemeal pitta breads
1/4 iceberg lettuce, shredded
Shredded red pepper and cucumber (optional)
4 tablespoons 0% fat Greek-style natural yogurt

1 Put half the onion, the garlic, the five spices and half the herbs into a food-processor and blend until thick and smooth. Pour into a bowl and combine with the chicken. Allow to marinate for 30–60 minutes or overnight.

2 Heat the olive oil in a non-stick frying pan and fry the other onion slices until soft. Remove the chicken from the marinade, scraping off the marinade (the more you leave on, the hotter the chicken will be) and add to the onion. Pan-fry until the chicken is cooked – about 5 minutes.

3 While the chicken is cooking, lightly toast the pitta bread on both sides. Split the side of each pitta to create a pocket. Put some lettuce in the bottom, fill with the chicken, red pepper and cucumber (if using) and top with a spoonful of yogurt and a sprinkling of the remaining mint and coriander.

Per portion: 422 kcal, 5g fat, 0.7g sat fat, 0.55g sodium, 64g carbohydrate

smoked salmon and cottage cheese sandwich

SERVES 1

2 slices wholegrain bread
Scraping of butter or low-fat spread (optional)
1/2 little gem lettuce, separated into leaves
Small handful of rocket
75g (3oz) low-fat soft cheese or cottage cheese
1/4 red onion, finely sliced
25g (1oz) thinly sliced smoked salmon
1 tablespoon capers
Ground black pepper

Spread both slices of bread with a little butter or low-fat spread if liked. Top one slice with lettuce, rocket, cheese, red onion, smoked salmon and capers, seasoning with pepper as you layer. Finish with the final slice of bread.

Per portion: 279 kcal, 5g fat, 1.3 sat fat, 1.18g sodium, 38g carbohydrate

vegetables

aromatic tomato tart

This exquisite tart is very simple to prepare and can be eaten either alone or as part of a main course. Tomatoes are low-GI and full of vitamin C. Cooking tomatoes, especially in olive oil, helps to release lycopene, an antioxidant and the reason why tomatoes are red.

SERVES 4

4 sheets filo pastry
2 tablespoons olive oil
1/2 teaspoon ground coriander
1/2 teaspoon fennel seeds
3 spring onions, sliced
1 teaspoon cumin seeds
2 garlic cloves, sliced
1/4 teaspoon chilli powder
6 large ripe tomatoes, each cut into 4 thick slices

1 Preheat the oven and a non-stick baking tray to 220°C/425°F/gas mark 7.

2 Lightly brush the sheets of filo pastry with a little of the olive oil and fold them in half. Stack them one on top of the other on another non-stick baking tray.

3 In a frying pan warm the rest of the oil over a medium heat. Add the ground coriander, fennel seeds, spring onions, cumin seeds and garlic, and stir-fry until the spices start releasing their fragrant bouquet. Add the chilli powder and the tomatoes (you will need to do this in two batches), and cook for 1–2 minutes, being careful not to break up the tomato slices. Set aside any cooking juices.

4 Arrange the tomatoes on the pastry, leaving a 5mm (1/4in) edge to the pastry. Set the baking tray on top of the hot tray in the oven and cook for 15–20 minutes, until the pastry is crisp and golden.

5 Drizzle any tomato spice juices over the tart and serve.

Per portion: 110 kcal, 8g fat, 1.6g sat fat, 0.04g sodium, 9g carbohydrate

barley and goat's cheese soufflé bake

Don't be afraid of this as it's more of a light vegetable bake than a true soufflé and it's not the least bit temperamental. Serve with tomato sauce (page 152) and a green salad.

SERVES 4

125g (4 1/2oz) brown wholegrain barley or pearl barley
1 tablespoon olive oil
1 medium onion, finely chopped
1 garlic clove, crushed
1 stick of celery, finely sliced
1 carrot, finely sliced
1/2 red pepper, finely chopped
1/4 teaspoon dried crushed chillies
3 egg whites
100g (3 1/2oz) goat's cheese, crumbled
Ground black pepper

1 Bring 350ml (12fl oz) water to the boil in a medium saucepan. Add the barley and simmer, covered, for 35–40 minutes, or until just tender. Drain and set aside.

2 Preheat the oven to 200°C/400°F/gas mark 6.

3 Heat the oil in a frying pan over a medium heat. Add the onion, cook for 5 minutes, then add the garlic, remaining vegetables and chillies and cook for a further 5 minutes.

4 Add the barley to the frying pan and toss with the vegetable mixture. Cook for 5 minutes, stirring occasionally. Transfer to a bowl and allow to cool.

5 In a large bowl, whisk the egg whites until soft peaks form – the mixture should be stiff, but not dry. Stir a third of the egg whites into the cooled barley mixture. Then fold in the remaining whites. Fold in the goat's cheese. Season with black pepper. Spoon the mixture into a buttered shallow ovenproof dish. Bake until golden, about 20 minutes.

Per portion: 226 kcal, 8g fat, 3.1g sat fat, 0.38g sodium, 33g carbohydrate

spaghetti with herby tomato sauce

This is a recipe with huge potential. This traditional sauce can be adapted according to your tastes and content of your cupboard – add capers, olives or mushrooms, or try replacing the sugar with a small piece of dark chocolate.

SERVES 3

1 tablespoon extra-virgin olive oil
1 small onion, finely diced
2 garlic cloves, finely diced
1 stick of celery, finely diced
500g (18oz) tomatoes, peeled and quartered
1 teaspoon raw cane sugar
150ml (1/4 pint) red wine
3 tablespoons torn basil leaves
1 tablespoon chopped parsley
250g (9oz) dried spaghetti
Salt and ground black pepper
25g (1oz) freshly grated parmesan

1 Heat the olive oil in a medium-sized saucepan and cook the onion, garlic and celery until soft but not brown. Add the tomatoes, sugar and red wine.

2 Cook for 20 minutes over a medium heat, stirring from time to time. Remove from the heat and stir in the basil and parsley. Meanwhile cook the spaghetti in plenty of fast-boiling water until al dente. Drain well.

3 Toss the spaghetti with the sauce, season to taste and top with the parmesan.

Per portion: 434 kcal, 9g fat, 2.4g sat fat, 0.32g sodium, 71g carbohydrate

spicy beans with carrot and coconut

Influenced by Indian cooking and full of wonderful spices and aromas, this recipe gives beans a much needed wake-up call. Lightly roasting the hazelnuts improves their flavour and if you are a vegetarian, the nuts are a good alternative source of iron. If you are allergic, leave them out and use vegetable oil instead.

SERVES 6–8

500g (18oz) extra-fine haricot verts (French beans), topped
2 tablespoons peanut or vegetable oil
1 teaspoon black mustard seeds
1 chilli, de-seeded and finely diced
2 small onions, finely sliced
2 garlic cloves, finely chopped
2 teaspoons grated ginger
1 teaspoon ground turmeric
1/4 teaspoon ground cardamom
110g (4oz) carrots, coarsely grated
175ml (6fl oz) vegetable stock
25g (1oz) desiccated coconut
25g (1oz) chopped roasted hazelnuts
2 tablespoons chopped coriander

1 Steam the beans for about 4 minutes until just tender, then set aside.

2 Heat the oil in a frying pan, add the mustard seeds, cover and cook over a medium heat until the seeds start to pop. Add the chilli, onions, garlic, ginger, turmeric and cardamom. Cook, stirring, for 4 minutes until the onions start to soften.

3 Add the carrots, stock and coconut and cook for 5 minutes.

4 Finally add the beans, hazelnuts and coriander and cook for 1–2 minutes to infuse the flavours and warm the beans.

5 Serve with rice or grilled or roast meats or fish.

Per portion: 124 kcal, 10g fat, 2.9g sat fat, 0.20g sodium, 7g carbohydrate

spicy braised aubergines with chickpeas & prunes

The prunes may surprise you but they add a touch of sweetness. Dried fruit is common in Middle Eastern dishes and increases the fibre and lowers the GI of a dish. Serve with basmati rice.

SERVES 4

2 large aubergines, cut in 2.5cm (1in) cubes
1 tablespoon vegetable oil
1 tablespoon sesame oil
1 tablespoon finely chopped garlic
1 tablespoon grated fresh ginger
2 bunches of spring onions, cut in 2.5cm (1in) batons
400g (14oz) tin of chickpeas, drained and rinsed
400ml (14fl oz) vegetable stock
1 tablespoon light soy sauce
175g (6oz) ready-to-eat 'stone-out' prunes, halved
2 teaspoons cornflour, mixed to a paste with a little water
2 tablespoons chopped coriander
1 chilli, de-seeded and finely diced

1 Toss the aubergine cubes in the vegetable oil in a shallow baking tray and place in a single layer under a preheated grill until lightly charred – this should take 10–15 minutes and they will need turning and shaking occasionally.

2 Heat the sesame oil in a large wok then add the garlic, ginger and spring onions and cook for 5 minutes, turning regularly. Add the aubergine to the pan, with the chickpeas, stock and soy and bring to the boil.

3 Add the prunes and cook for a further 10 minutes. Add the cornflour and stir to thicken. Pour the mixture into a dish and sprinkle with the coriander and chilli.

Per portion: 223 kcal, 8g fat, 1.0g sat fat, 0.44g sodium, 31g carbohydrate

oriental greens with oyster sauce

Choose 'strong' greens such as pak choy, Swiss chard, spinach or any of the Oriental greens available in Chinese markets. This easy recipe brings out the sweetness of the vegetables in the blanching process while the sauce adds a rich, almost nutty flavour.

SERVES 4

500g (18oz) Oriental greens, leaves separated and roughly chopped if wished
1 teaspoon sesame oil
1 teaspoon groundnut or vegetable oil
1cm (1/2in) piece of fresh root ginger, peeled and finely grated
1 red chilli, de-seeded and finely diced
1 garlic clove, finely chopped
2 tablespoons oyster sauce
2 tablespoons Chinese rice wine (Mirin) or dry sherry
2 tablespoons light soy sauce
1/2 tablespoon liquid honey

1 Bring a large pan of water to a rolling boil, add the greens and blanch for 1–3 minutes, depending on the vegetable you are using, until wilted and just tender but still with a bite. Drain well and place on a warm serving dish. Keep warm.

2 Meanwhile, heat the sesame and the groundnut or vegetable oil in a small frying pan. Add the ginger, chilli and garlic and cook for 2 minutes, stirring, then stir in the oyster sauce, Mirin or sherry, soy and honey. Just heat through and drizzle over the greens to serve.

Per portion: 90 kcal, 3g fat, 0.4g sat fat, 0.34g sodium, 9g carbohydrate

grilled vegetable pizza

SERVES 4 – MAKES 1 X 35CM (14IN) PIZZA OR 2 X 23CM (9IN)

Wholegrain pizza dough
250g (9oz) wholegrain flour
1 sachet easy-blend yeast
Pinch of sugar
1/2 teaspoon salt
1 tablespoon olive oil

4 plum tomatoes, cut into rough chunks
110g (4oz) wood-roasted onions, halved if large
110g (4oz) grilled artichokes, drained and quartered
110g (4oz) wood-roasted red peppers, drained and sliced
1 tablespoon oregano leaves
110g (4oz) ricotta
Small handful of rocket leaves
25g (1oz) pine nuts, toasted

1 To make the pizza dough, combine the flour, yeast, sugar, salt, olive oil and about 150ml (1/4 pint) hand-hot water and mix well with a wooden spoon.

2 Turn out on to a work surface and knead for 7–10 minutes, until smooth and elastic. The dough should feel moist to the touch. You can use an electric mixer with a dough hook – mix for 5–7 minutes – or a food-processor for 1 minute.

3 Place the dough in a lightly oiled bowl and turn to coat the top with oil. Cover with clingfilm and leave to rise in a warm place for 30–60 minutes until doubled in size.

4 Preheat the oven to 220°C/425°F/gas mark 7. Roll out the pizza base and scatter the vegetables and oregano over. Dot with ricotta and season with pepper. Bake for about 15 minutes. Scatter with rocket leaves and pine nuts and serve at once.

Per portion – pizza topping: 137 kcal, 8g fat, 2.3g sat fat, 0.06g sodium, 12g carbohydrate
Per portion – pizza dough: 344 kcal, 17g fat, 2.4g sat fat, 0.25g sodium, 44g carbohydrate

corn pudding

This also makes a good quiche filling – line a quiche tin or shallow cake tin with very thinly rolled out wholegrain bread dough (see recipe, left) and bake as below.

SERVES 6

10g (1/2oz) unsalted butter
1 small onion, finely chopped
1 garlic clove, finely chopped
1 teaspoon thyme leaves
1/2 green pepper, finely chopped
2 green chillies, de-seeded and finely diced
Corn kernels from 3 ears of corn or 250g (9oz) frozen or
   tinned corn kernels, thawed and well drained
1/2 teaspoon each of ground black pepper and ground nutmeg
Pinch of cayenne pepper
2 tablespoons cornflour
425ml (3/4 pint) semi-skimmed milk
3 eggs
2 tablespoons chopped flat-leaf parsley
1 tablespoon snipped chives
50g (2oz) freshly grated parmesan
50g (2oz) Gruyère cheese, grated

1 Preheat the oven to 180°C/350°F/ gas mark 4.

2 Heat the butter in a frying pan, add the onion, garlic, thyme, green pepper and chillies. Cook over a medium heat for 3 minutes. Add half the corn and cook for 5 minutes (2–3 if using frozen or tinned). Set aside then season with pepper, nutmeg and cayenne.

3 Place the remaining corn in a liquidiser with the cornflour, milk and eggs and whizz until smooth. Fold in the corn mixture, herbs and both cheeses.

4 Pour into a baking dish, place in a hot bain-marie and cook until firm, about 1 hour. Let it stand for 10 minutes before serving. Eat as it is or serve cold with meats and salad.

Per portion: 237 kcal, 13g fat, 6.5g sat fat, 0.23g sodium, 18g carbohydrate

dal with added spice

Lentils are naturally rich in protein. The body deals efficiently with protein found in meat, fish and dairy products but the vegetable proteins found in lentils require more effort to digest, so the Indians added certain digestion-friendly spices such as ginger and asafoetida. Serve with flatbread or basmati rice.

SERVES 4–6

250g (9oz) red lentils, washed
25g (1oz) ghee or clarified butter
5 garlic cloves, finely chopped
1 onion, finely chopped
2.5cm (1in) piece of ginger, finely chopped
3 green chillies, de-seeded and finely chopped
1 teaspoon ground coriander
1 teaspoon ground cumin
1/2 teaspoon chilli powder
1 teaspoon black mustard seeds
1 teaspoon turmeric
Pinch of asafoetida (optional)
3 plum tomatoes, de-seeded and diced
3 tablespoons chopped coriander
2 tablespoons lime juice

1 Pour 600ml (1 pint) water in a saucepan over a medium heat, add the lentils and cook for 15 minutes, stirring regularly at first as it is during the early period of cooking that the lentils will stick together.

2 Meanwhile, heat the ghee in a frying pan and add the garlic, onion, ginger and chillies and cook for 10 minutes over a medium heat until the onion has softened. Add the spices and cook for a further 2 minutes. Fold into the lentils.

3 Cook the dal for 10–15 minutes, adding a little boiling water if necessary until the lentils are tender and the mixture is slightly sloppy. Fold in the tomatoes, coriander and lime juice.

Per portion: 286 kcal, 8g fat, 4.3g sat fat, 0.03g sodium, 41g carbohydrate

oriental tofu, onion and mushroom kebabs

These are great kebabs for the barbecue or grill. Tofu is fermented soya bean curd, which not only contains protein but is also full of beneficial phytoestrogens. Serve with brown rice.

SERVES 4

75ml (3fl oz) light soy sauce
75ml (3fl oz) fresh unsweetened orange juice
1 tablespoon rice vinegar
1 tablespoon sesame oil
1 garlic clove, finely chopped
2 tablespoons chopped coriander
2 tablespoons finely chopped ginger
1/2 teaspoon finely chopped chilli
1 head pak choy
450g (1lb) firm tofu, drained and cut in 2.5cm (1in) cubes
20 shiitake or button mushrooms
1 red onion, cut lengthways into 8 wedges
Wooden skewers, soaked in water for about 30 minutes

1 Prepare the marinade by combining the first eight ingredients.

2 Separate the pak choy leaves and cut the stems into 2.5cm (1in) sections. Marinate with the tofu, mushrooms and onion for up to 1 hour, depending on how strong a flavour you want.

3 Thread the ingredients (you'll need to roll the pak choy leaves) onto four large (or twelve small) thick wooden skewers, and cook on a barbecue or under a grill for 7–10 minutes, basting with the marinade and turning regularly.

Per portion: 242 kcal, 8g fat, 1.0g sat fat, 0.02g sodium, 28g carbohydrate

courgette, sun-dried tomato and basil frittata

This is a fantastic egg-based dish that is full of Mediterranean flavour and goodness. Serve in wedges, warm or at room temperature.

SERVES 4

1 tablespoon extra-virgin olive oil
1 onion, finely sliced
1 teaspoon soft thyme leaves
1 large courgette, halved lengthways and finely sliced
50g (2oz) sun-dried tomatoes, chopped
1/2 x 400g (14oz) tin borlotti or kidney beans (tinned in water), drained and rinsed
3 tablespoons torn basil leaves
6 eggs, lightly beaten
Ground black pepper

1 Heat half the oil in a 23cm (9in) non-stick frying pan and cook the onion and thyme over a medium heat until the onion has softened but still colourless. Add the courgette and cook for a further 3–5 minutes until tender.

2 Pour the mixture into a colander to drain and cool, then combine with the sun-dried tomatoes, beans and basil. Add this mixture to the beaten egg, and season with ground black pepper.

3 Wipe the frying pan with kitchen paper, then pour in the remaining oil and place over a medium heat. When the oil is hot enough to make the egg sizzle, pour in the mixture. Stir with a fork for a couple of minutes to ensure that the pan is evenly covered. Reduce the heat and cook the frittata gently until the base is lightly set, about 10 minutes.

4 Slide the frittata on to a large plate then invert back into the frying pan and cook for a further 5 minutes until just firm.

Per portion: 269 kcal, 19g fat, 3.9g sat fat, 0.36g sodium, 11g carbohydrate

chickpea curry

Try making this curry instead of a dal. Like all savoury stews it is best eaten the day after making, so that the flavours have time to mellow.

SERVES 6–8

250g (9oz) dried chickpeas, soaked overnight then drained
  and rinsed
2.5cm (1in) piece of ginger, sliced
3 bay leaves
7.5cm (3in) piece of cinnamon stick
3 large onions, roughly chopped
2 tablespoons olive oil
1 tablespoon finely chopped garlic
1 tablespoon grated ginger
1 teaspoon ground turmeric
2 chillies, de-seeded and finely sliced
400g (14oz) tin of chopped tomatoes
2 crushed black or green cardamoms
6 whole cloves
1 teaspoon black peppercorns
1 teaspoon cumin seeds, toasted
1 cauliflower, broken into florets
225g (8oz) bag washed spinach
1 tablespoon garam masala
1 tablespoon chopped mint
2 tablespoons chopped coriander

1 Cook the chickpeas with the sliced ginger, bay leaves, two-thirds of the cinnamon stick and half the onion in about 2 litres (3½ pints) water until tender. This will take about 1–2 hours, depending on the age of the chickpeas. Drain, reserving the liquid, and discard the ginger, bay and cinnamon.

2 Meanwhile, 45 minutes before the chickpeas have finished cooking, blend the remaining onions in a food-processor. Heat the olive oil in a large saucepan, then cook the onions with the garlic and ginger until the onions have softened but not yet coloured.

3 Add the turmeric and chillies and cook for a further 3 minutes. Add the tinned tomatoes and half of the reserved cooking liquid and bring to the boil.

4 Tie the remaining cinnamon, cardamoms, cloves, peppercorns and cumin in muslin or cheesecloth and add to the tomatoes. Bring to a simmer then add the cauliflower and cook for about 20 minutes.

5 Add the spinach, stir to combine, and cook until the spinach has wilted. Add the drained chickpeas and simmer for a further 15 minutes. Add as much of the remaining chickpea cooking liquid as required to give the preferred consistency. Remove and squeeze the juices from the muslin. Stir in the garam masala, mint and coriander.

6 Serve with brown basmati rice or wholemeal chapatis.

Per portion: 186 kcal, 7g fat, 0.9g sat fat, 0.09g sodium, 23g carbohydrate

baked potato skins

Simply irresistible, these will make your mouth water as they cook. Eat with sweetcorn or refried or baked beans for a nutritious, low-GI snack.

SERVES 4

6 potatoes or sweet potatoes, each about 175g (6oz)
1 tablespoon olive oil
Salt and ground black pepper
1 tablespoon finely chopped rosemary

1 Preheat the oven to 200°C/400°F/gas mark 6.

2 Prick each potato all over and place them directly on the oven shelf. Bake for 40–45 minutes or until slightly softened when squeezed, then leave to cool.

3 Cut each potato in half lengthways and then in half again. Slice away a bit of the flesh, leaving a layer of potato at least 5mm (1/4in) thick on the skin. Brush the skins with oil then arrange in a single layer, skin side down on a wire rack set on a roasting tin. Season and sprinkle over the rosemary. Bake for about 30 minutes until crisp and golden brown. Serve hot.

Per portion: 222 kcal, 3g fat, 0.4g sat fat, 0.22g sodium, 45g carbohydrate

corn and pepper bake

This is a really satisfying dish based on a traditional southern American recipe. Serve with wholegrain bread or grilled chicken.

SERVES 6

1 tablespoon olive oil
2 leeks, shredded
1 red pepper, de-seeded and chopped
400g (14oz) frozen sweetcorn, thawed and well drained
Ground black pepper
4 eggs
1 teaspoon English mustard
600ml (1 pint) semi-skimmed milk
1/2 teaspoon Tabasco sauce
1/2 teaspoon Worcestershire sauce

1 Preheat the oven to 180°C/ 350°F/gas mark 4.

2 Heat the oil in a large saucepan and cook the leeks, red pepper and corn for 5 minutes. Season generously with black pepper and pour the mixture into a baking dish.

3 In a bowl, beat together the eggs, mustard, milk, Tabasco and Worcestershire sauces. Pour over the sweetcorn mix. Bake in a hot bain-marie for 35–40 minutes or until a knife comes out clean when inserted into the centre.

Per portion: 148 kcal, 8g fat, 2.5g sat fat, 0.79g sodium, 9g carbohydrate

fish

seared swordfish with salsa fresca

Swordfish are found in temperate as well as tropical waters and are extremely popular in the US. Best grilled, this meaty fish isn't overpowered by the spicy salsa. Serve with new potatoes in their skins and a green salad.

SERVES 4

1 teaspoon olive oil
1 garlic clove, finely chopped
1 red chilli, de-seeded and finely chopped
1/2 teaspoon ground cumin
1/2 teaspoon ground coriander
Juice of 1 lime
Ground black pepper
4 x 125g (41/2oz) swordfish steaks
125g (41/2oz) tiny cherry tomatoes, halved
1 ripe, firm avocado, peeled, stoned and chopped
1 very small red onion, finely chopped
2 tablespoons chopped fresh coriander

1 Place the oil in a shallow non-metallic dish with the garlic, half the chilli, half the ground cumin and half the ground coriander. Add the juice of half a lime and season with pepper. Stir well, then add the swordfish steaks, turning to coat. Cover with clingfilm and marinate for 30 minutes to allow the flavours to develop.

2 To make the salsa, place the remaining chilli, ground cumin, coriander and lime juice in a bowl. Add the cherry tomatoes, avocado, red onion and fresh coriander and mix gently to combine. Set aside.

3 Heat a griddle pan. Remove the swordfish steaks from the marinade. Add to the pan and chargrill for 1–2 minutes on each side or until well seared and just tender.

4 Spoon some salsa over the swordfish and serve at once.

Per portion: 226 kcal, 13g fat, 2.8g sat fat, 0.17g sodium, 3g carbohydrate

seared tuna sashimi with spicy lentil salad

In Japan, sashimi is a dish of sliced raw fish that is traditionally presented on a pile of shredded radish with wasabi and a dipping sauce. Here, the tuna is lightly seared and served on a bed of lentils. Lentils contain considerably more protein than any other vegetable as well as being full of fibre. Adding them to a dish will lower the GI. Pregnant women, nursing mothers and the elderly are not advised to eat raw fish.

SERVES 4–6

10g (1/2oz) black peppercorns, quite finely ground and mixed with 1/4 teaspoon powdered star anise
450g (1lb) very fresh trimmed tuna loin (preferably sashimi grade, otherwise buy from a good fishmonger), in a piece
2–4 teaspoons wasabi paste (Japanese green horseradish)
6 tablespoons reduced-calorie mayonnaise

Spicy lentil salad
250g (9oz) Puy lentils, washed
Vegetable stock or water
3 garlic cloves
11/2 red onions, finely diced
Finely grated zest and juice of 1 lime
1 tablespoon extra-virgin olive oil
4 large red chillies, chargrilled or roasted, de-seeded and chopped
Coriander leaves, to garnish

Dipping sauce
5 tablespoons light soy sauce
1/2 teaspoon juices from grated fresh ginger
1/2 teaspoon wasabi paste

1 Place the black pepper mix in a shallow tray and roll the tuna in it, pressing the pepper into the flesh. Heat a thick-based frying pan without fat over a high heat until extremely hot. Place the tuna in the pan and sear each side until the heat has penetrated 5mm (1/4in) all around. The pepper will be nicely charred and aromatic. Set aside and, when cool, refrigerate until ready to serve.

2 Mix the wasabi paste into the mayonnaise until the desired fieriness is achieved.

3 To make the lentil salad, put the lentils in a saucepan and add the stock or water until it covers the lentils by about 2.5cm (1in). Cook with the whole garlic over a medium heat for 20–25 minutes until just tender. Drain, discard the garlic and fold in the remaining ingredients.

4 To make the dipping sauce, mix the ingredients together with 5 tablespoons iced water and leave for 30 minutes.

5 Remove the tuna from the fridge and cut it into 8mm (¹/₃in) slices using a simple, single draw from top to bottom with a long, sharp knife. The flesh of the tuna will cut like butter so do not be tempted to use a sawing motion.

6 To serve, place a heap of lentils on each plate. Lean the slices of tuna against the lentils. Garnish with coriander leaves and serve with the dipping sauce and wasabi mayonnaise.

Per portion: 494 kcal, 18g fat, 3.2g sat fat, 0.52g sodium, 41g carbohydrate

grilled tuna with celeriac skordalia and rocket

Skordalia is a Greek garlic sauce, usually made with bread or potatoes. The key to making it successfully is to add the olive oil slowly. I've added celeriac as well, as it is a lovely mild, slightly sweet-tasting vegetable that is full of fibre and goes really well with potatoes.

SERVES 4

4 tuna loin steaks, about 125g (4 1/2oz) each
1 tablespoon extra-virgin olive oil
Ground black pepper
4 handfuls rocket leaves, washed and dried
4 lemon wedges

Celeriac skordalia
350g (12oz) prepared celeriac, cubed
110g (4oz) new potatoes, unpeeled and cubed
5 garlic cloves, finely chopped
1 tablespoon lemon juice or white wine vinegar
2 tablespoons extra-virgin olive oil
Ground black pepper

1 For the skordalia, steam the celeriac and potatoes for about 20 minutes until tender. Soak the garlic in the lemon juice.

2 Put the warm vegetables in a food-processor and blend until smooth. With the machine running, add the garlic and slowly pour in the oil as if you were making a mayonnaise. Season to taste with the pepper and the lemon juice.

3 To cook the tuna, preheat a ridged grill pan. Rub the tuna lightly with olive oil and pepper. Cook for 1–2 minutes on each side, depending on how rare you like the tuna. (It's up to you, but I think well-done tuna is a waste and you may as well just open a tin.)

4 Serve the tuna on the celeriac skordalia with the rocket on the side and a wedge of lemon.

Per portion: 300 kcal, 15g fat, 2.9g sat fat, 0.14g sodium, 9g carbohydrate

pan-fried mullet with olives and tomatoes

Quick and easy, this is a perfect supper recipe. Although this dish is based on Mediterranean cooking, red mullet is also found in the Atlantic. Serve with new potatoes in their skins and green beans.

SERVES 2

2 tablespoons black olive purée
2 medium-sized red mullet, filleted
1 tablespoon extra-virgin olive oil
250g (9oz) tomatoes, de-seeded and diced
4 teaspoons coarsely chopped tarragon or chervil
1 tablespoon chopped basil
Ground black pepper
Juice of 1/2–1 lime

1 Spread the olive purée on the flesh side of the fish.

2 Heat the olive oil in a non-stick frying pan and cook the fillets, skin side up, for 3 minutes. Turn the fillets over and cook for a further 3 minutes. Remove and keep warm.

3 Combine the tomatoes, herbs and pepper and warm through in the frying pan, adding lime juice to taste. Pour this dressing over the red mullet, and serve.

Per portion: 186 kcal, 10g fat, 1.0g sat fat, 0.22g sodium, 4g carbohydrate

spaghetti with anchovies and parsley

This dish is packed with taste but is really easy to make. Perfect for when you want a quick meal, this is also a great storecupboard standby.

SERVES 4

350g (12oz) dried spaghetti
6 garlic cloves, smashed roughly with the back of a knife
50g (2oz) tinned anchovies, chopped – reserve the oil
2 chillies, de-seeded and finely sliced
6 tablespoons chopped parsley
2 tablespoons dry white wine
$^1/_2$–1 teaspoon ground black pepper

1 Cook the spaghetti in plenty of boiling water until cooked but still *al dente*. When the pasta is cooked, drain and return to the pan, reserving a little pasta water.

2 Meanwhile, fry the garlic, anchovies and chillies in the reserved olive oil from the tin in a medium frying pan over a gentle heat for about 10 minutes until the garlic is golden.

3 Add the parsley, white wine, pepper and 4 tablespoons pasta water to deglaze the pan.

4 Pour the anchovy mixture over the pasta and toss to combine, adding a little extra reserved water if necessary.

Per portion: 347 kcal, 4g fat, 0.0g sat fat, 0.50g sodium, 66g carbohydrate

herbed trout with fennel

Trout is an excellent source of omega-3 fatty acids, and is also full of flavour. It needs nothing more than a few salad leaves and lemon to accompany it.

SERVES 2

4 sprigs of rosemary
4 sprigs of fennel fronds
4 sprigs of parsley
4 sprigs of oregano
2 medium-sized trout, gutted
1 tablespoon olive oil
Ground black pepper
2 small heads fennel, cut in 2 lengthways
Handful of rocket leaves
Lemon wedges

1 Preheat the oven to 190°C/375°F/gas mark 5.

2 Place the herbs inside the trout and tie with fine string or secure with wooden cocktail sticks.

3 Arrange the fish in a shallow roasting tin. Drizzle the olive oil over the fish and season with pepper.

4 Blanch the fennel in boiling water for 10 minutes, then drain and place next to the trout. Brown the trout and fennel over a medium heat on top of the stove, turning once, then transfer to the oven for about 15 minutes to finish cooking.

5 Serve the trout with the fennel and pour over any cooking juices, together with some rocket leaves and lemon wedges.

Per portion: 363 kcal, 18g fat, 3.3g sat fat, 0.12g sodium, 4g carbohydrate

smoked haddock, salmon and prawn pie with a spinach topping

A fish pie is one of the most comforting meals and this version is no exception. Full of aromatic herbs and spices with a golden cheesey top, I make this when I need a really filling meal. The mashed potato has been combined with spinach to bring down the GI, add a good source of iron and fibre and give it a lovely speckly appearance.

SERVES 6

500g (18oz) floury potatoes, such as Maris Piper, cut
   into chunks
500g (18oz) frozen spinach, thawed and thoroughly drained
700ml (1¼ pints) skimmed milk
Grated fresh nutmeg
Ground black pepper
2 fresh bay leaves
1 whole clove
250g (9oz) salmon fillet (in one piece)
250g (9oz) haddock fillet (in one piece)
25g (1oz) unsalted butter
1 onion, finely diced
25g (1oz) cornflour
1 teaspoon anchovy essence
2 tablespoons chopped parsley
½ teaspoon soft thyme leaves
1 teaspoon dry English mustard powder
200g (7oz) large peeled prawns (raw or cooked)
50g (2oz) Gruyère, grated
25g (1oz) freshly grated parmesan
Sugar snap peas
Roasted cherry tomatoes

1 Preheat the oven to 200°C/400°F/gas mark 6.

2 To make the topping, steam the potatoes for 15–20 minutes or until completely tender. Drain and return to the pan with the thawed spinach over a gentle heat for a couple of minutes to dry out, shaking the pan occasionally to prevent the potatoes sticking to the bottom. Mash the potatoes then beat in up to 100ml (3½fl oz) milk and season to taste with nutmeg and pepper.

3 Place 600ml (1 pint) milk in a sauté pan with the bay leaves, clove and a pinch of nutmeg. Add the salmon and haddock fillets and poach for 6–8 minutes or until the fish is just tender. Transfer the fish fillets to a plate with a fish slice and set aside until they are cool enough to handle, then flake the flesh, discarding the skin and any bones. Set aside. Strain the poaching liquid and set aside.

4 Melt the butter in a large non-stick pan. Add the onion and cook for 6–8 minutes until the onion has softened but not coloured, stirring occasionally. Pour in the reserved poaching milk. Mix the cornflour to a paste with the remaining milk then add a little warm milk from the pan and return to the rest of the liquid, stirring all the time. Reduce the heat and simmer gently for 10 minutes, stirring occasionally until slightly reduced and thickened.

5 Stir the anchovy essence, parsley, thyme and mustard powder into the sauce. Fold in the reserved flaked fish and prawns, then season to taste. Spoon the fish mixture into an ovenproof dish, that is at least 2.25 litres (4 pints) in size. Allow a light skin to form, then carefully spread over the spinach and potato mash to cover. Smooth over with a palette knife and fluff up with a fork. Mix together the Gruyère and parmesan and sprinkle over the top, then bake for 20–25 minutes or until the cheese is bubbling and golden.

6 Serve at once with the vegetables.

Per portion: 370 kcal, 14g fat, 5.9g sat fat, 0.41g sodium, 28g carbohydrate

crab and asparagus fettuccine

Pasta is one of the best GI foods. Low in fat, it will also fill you up and prevent late-night snacking. White crab meat comes from the claws, but you can also use brown meat – it has a more intense flavour.

SERVES 4

2 tablespoons extra-virgin olive oil
1 shallot, finely diced
1 tablespoon lemon thyme leaves
2 teaspoons anchovy essence
150ml (¼ pint) dry white wine
150ml (¼ pint) fish stock
350g (12oz) asparagus, trimmed and cut into 2.5cm
    (1in) pieces
250g (9oz) white crab meat
400g (14oz) fresh fettuccine
10g (½oz) unsalted butter
Juice of 1 lemon
4 tablespoons chopped parsley
Ground black pepper

1 Heat the olive oil in a heavy-bottomed frying pan, add the shallot and cook gently until soft but not brown. Add the thyme, anchovy essence, wine and fish stock and bring to the boil. Reduce to a simmer.

2 Meanwhile bring a large pot of water to the boil. Add the asparagus and cook for 4–6 minutes until just tender. Drain, reserving the cooking water, and add the asparagus to the shallot liquid with the crab.

3 Cook the fettuccine in the asparagus water for 3–4 minutes. Drain and add to the crab sauce.

4 Heat the butter in a frying pan until nutty and golden, add the lemon juice and parsley and pour over the pasta. Toss to combine. Season to taste with plenty of black pepper.

Per portion: 476 kcal, 16g fat, 3.3g sat fat, 0.74g sodium, 50g carbohydrate

thai steamed salmon

Here the salmon is marinated in coriander, ginger, mint, lime juice and chillies. Serve with brown basmati rice or rice noodles and steamed green beans or pak choy.

SERVES 4

Small bunch of coriander, washed
12 mint leaves, washed
$1/2$ teaspoon salt
2 garlic cloves, crushed
2 green chillies, de-seeded and chopped
3 tablespoons fresh lime juice
1 tablespoon golden caster sugar
1 teaspoon peeled and chopped ginger
1 tablespoon fish sauce (Nam Pla)
4 x 125g (4$1/2$oz) salmon fillets

1 In a food-processor blend together the coriander leaves and stalks, mint leaves, salt, garlic and chillies to make a rough paste. Add the lime juice, caster sugar, ginger and fish sauce and process until fairly smooth. Spoon the sauce into a heatproof bowl and combine with the salmon, then marinate for 20 minutes.

2 Boil some water in the bottom half of a steamer. Place the bowl with the marinated salmon in the top half and steam for 6–8 minutes.

3 Serve immediately with the rice or noodles and vegetables.

Per portion: 254 kcal, 14g fat, 2.4g sat fat, 0.37g sodium, 7g carbohydrate

thai fish cakes with cucumber relish

SERVES 4

500g (18oz) cod fillet, skinned
25g (1oz) fresh coriander, chopped
2–3 tablespoons red curry paste
1 teaspoon cornflour mixed with 1 tablespoon lime juice
1 egg white
2 spring onions, finely chopped
Oil spray, for frying

Cucumber relish
100ml (3¹/2fl oz) rice vinegar
2 tablespoons golden caster sugar
10cm (4in) piece cucumber, unpeeled
1 small carrot
1 shallot, finely sliced
1 red chilli, de-seeded and finely sliced
2 tablespoons roasted peanuts, roughly chopped

1 To make the relish, boil the vinegar and sugar until the sugar dissolves, simmer for 1–2 minutes, then leave to cool.

2 Quarter the cucumber lengthways, de-seed then slice crossways finely. Halve the carrot lengthways and slice thinly.

3 Add the cucumber, carrot, shallot and chilli to the cold syrup and mix. Leave for 4 hours. Add the peanuts before serving.

4 Put all the ingredients for the fish cakes except the spring onions and oil in a food-processor and whizz until the mixture forms a smoothish paste. Remove from the food-processor and work in the spring onions.

5 Spray a non-stick frying pan with oil and cook a small amount of the mixture to check the seasoning. If you like, add more curry paste, then shape the mixture into 12 small cakes. Fry the fish cakes for about 3 minutes each side until cooked through. Serve warm with the relish.

Per portion: 239 kcal, 8g fat, 1.1g sat fat, 0.25g sodium, 15g carbohydrate

mussels with bacon

This is full of wonderful tastes and aromas. Serve with wholegrain bread or brown basmati rice to soak up all the cooking liquor, and a leaf salad.

SERVES 4

150ml (¹/4 pint) dry cider
2kg (4¹/2lb) fresh mussels, cleaned and beards removed
4 slices back bacon, cut in thin strips
¹/2 onion, finely diced
6 sage leaves, finely chopped
1 red apple, cored and diced
Ground black pepper

1 In a very large saucepan, bring the cider to a fast boil, add the mussels and cover with a lid. Cook for 3–5 minutes, shaking the pan occasionally until the mussels open. Discard any that remain closed. Remove about half the mussels from their shells if wished, reserving the cooking liquid.

2 Strain the mussel liquor, return to the heat, add the mussels and keep on the gentlest simmer.

3 Meanwhile, in a frying pan, cook the bacon with the onion and sage until the bacon is crisp. Add the apple and cook for a further 2–3 minutes. Season with ground black pepper.

4 Divide the mussels with their liquor between four warm bowls. Sprinkle over with the bacon mix and eat with warm wholegrain bread or brown basmati rice.

Per portion: 252 kcal, 7g fat, 1.8g sat fat, 1.13g sodium, 10g carbohydrate

grilled mackerel with chilli and horseradish

Fresh mackerel can be quite hard to find, but well worth the effort. It is a beautiful-looking fish with silver-grey markings and a fantastic flavour. It also contains more omega-3 fatty acids than any other fish. Serve with new potatoes in their skins and a green vegetable or salad.

SERVES 4

4 very fresh small whole mackerel, heads removed, gutted
   and well cleaned
1 tablespoon de-seeded and diced red chilli
Ground black pepper
1 tablespoon olive oil
4 spring onions, finely sliced
4 teaspoons grated horseradish (not creamed)
1 teaspoon dried chilli flakes
2 teaspoons chopped rosemary leaves
Juice of 2 lemons

1 Slash the mackerel twice on each side, and place a little chilli in each cut. Season with black pepper and rub with the olive oil.

2 Place the fish under a hot grill or on a barbecue (weather permitting). Cook for 5–7 minutes each side or until the skin is crispy and the fish is cooked through.

3 Meanwhile mix the spring onions, horseradish, dried chilli and rosemary, then add the lemon juice and a dash of water to give a pouring consistency.

4 Drizzle over the mackerel and serve.

Per portion: 249 kcal, 19g fat, 3.7g sat fat, 0.08g sodium, 1g carbohydrate

chargrilled squid with marinated chicory

Scoring the squid before cooking not only makes the finished result look more professional, it also helps the squid to cook through quickly and the shorter the cooking time the more tender the end result will be.

SERVES 4

200ml (7fl oz) cider vinegar
40g (1¹/₂oz) caster sugar
1 chilli, sliced in 2
Sprig of thyme
1 bay leaf
1 teaspoon black peppercorns, crushed
1 teaspoon juniper berries, crushed
4 heads red or green chicory
2 tablespoons extra-virgin olive oil
3 tablespoons chopped flat-leaf parsley
Ground black pepper
400g (14oz) prepared and cleaned squid
2 teaspoons chopped fresh red chilli

1 Pour 900ml (1¹/₂ pints) water into a non-reactive saucepan, add the vinegar, sugar and flavourings and bring to the boil. Add the chicory to this marinade and cook for 10 minutes.

2 Drain well, then cut the chicory in half lengthways. Drizzle the chicory with half the oil and scatter with parsley. Season to taste with black pepper and allow to cool to room temperature.

3 Lightly slash the squid at 1cm (½in) intervals without cutting all the way through.

4 Toss the squid in the remaining oil, then place it on a preheated ridged griddle pan and cook for no more than 1 minute each side, depending on its thickness. Season with pepper and sprinkle with the chopped chilli. Serve with the chicory.

Per portion: 196 kcal, 8g fat, 1.3g sat fat, 0.13g sodium, 13g carbohydrate

meat and poultry

spicy chicken fillets

You need to marinate the chicken overnight in the spices, but it is worth planning ahead as the marinade keeps the chicken from drying out under the grill and gives it lots of flavour.

SERVES 4

4 garlic cloves, crushed
150ml (1/4 pint) low-fat natural yogurt
1 tablespoon grated onion
1 chilli, de-seeded and finely diced
1 teaspoon each of ground coriander, cumin, fenugreek,
* paprika and ginger*
Pinch of dry mustard powder
4 chicken breast fillets, cut in large strips
Lime wedges

1 Mix together the garlic, yogurt, onion, chilli, spices and mustard. Add the chicken and marinate overnight.

2 Scrape most of the yogurt from the chicken, and chargrill or grill for 3–4 minutes on each side.

3 Serve with the lime wedges, brown basmati rice and a green vegetable or salad. Cold, the chicken makes a great filling for sandwiches and tortilla wraps.

Per portion: 163 kcal, 2g fat, 0.6g sat fat, 0.11g sodium, 4g carbohydrate

simple roast chicken

Here is one of the easiest methods of roasting poultry, where the butter makes the skin crisp and golden. Allow the chicken to rest for 15 minutes before serving to give it time to reabsorb the juices released, so that the meat will be tender and delicious. Serve with baked sweet potatoes and green vegetables. See also page 133 for another great roast recipe.

SERVES 6

1 large free-range chicken (about 1.5kg/3lb 5oz)
10g (1/2oz) unsalted butter, melted
Several grindings of black pepper
2 sprigs of thyme
1–2 garlic heads, broken into cloves
175ml (6fl oz) dry white wine

1 Preheat the oven to 220°C/425°F/gas mark 7.

2 Brush the chicken with the butter, then sprinkle with black pepper. Pop the thyme into the cavity of the chicken. Put into a roasting tray with the garlic cloves and the white wine and roast in the oven for 20 minutes.

3 Reduce the heat to 190°C/375°F/gas mark 5 and roast for a further 45 minutes, basting from time to time. Turn off the oven, but leave the chicken in it to rest for 15 minutes before carving and serving with the juices.

Per portion: 127 kcal, 3g fat, 1.4g sat fat, 0.07g sodium, 1g carbohydrate

moroccan lamb stew with pumpkin and pickled lemon

This is one of my favourite recipes, full of colour and flavour. Harissa and pickled lemons are an integral part of North African cooking and are a perfect foil for lamb in this satisfying dish. Serve with bulgur wheat or warmed flatbread.

SERVES 4

450g (1lb) lean leg of lamb, cut into 2.5cm (1in) cubes
1¹/₂ teaspoons ground black pepper
1 teaspoon olive oil
1 large onion, roughly diced
4 garlic cloves, crushed
4 tomatoes, skinned and diced
1 tablespoon harissa or hot pepper paste
400g (14oz) tin of chickpeas in water, drained and rinsed
350g (12oz) trimmed and peeled pumpkin, cut
*   into 2.5cm (1in) cubes*
1 pickled lemon, finely diced
2 tablespoons chopped mint
1 tablespoon chopped coriander

1 Coat the lamb in the black pepper.

2 Heat the oil in a large non-stick saucepan, add the lamb and cook until it has browned all over. Add the onion and garlic and cook until the onion is soft and is slightly brown, adding a splash of water if necessary to prevent sticking.

3 Add the tomatoes, harissa and 425ml (³/₄ pint) water. Bring to a simmer, cover and cook over a medium heat for 1¹/₄–1¹/₂ hours, topping up with water as necessary, until the lamb is almost tender.

4 Add the chickpeas and pumpkin and cook for a further 15 minutes or until the pumpkin is tender. Add the lemon, mint and coriander. Serve immediately.

Per portion: 357 kcal, 18g fat, 6.6g sat fat, 0.28g sodium, 21g carbohydrate

sausage patties with lentils

If you are partial to bangers and mash, try this. Instead of mashed potatoes, the lentils make a really flavoursome low-GI accompaniment.

SERVES 4

110g (4oz) smoked back bacon, chopped
1 carrot, chopped
1 stick of celery, chopped
1 onion, chopped
4 garlic cloves, finely chopped
2 teaspoons soft fresh thyme leaves
1 bay leaf
700ml (1¼ pints) chicken stock
50g (2oz) dried ceps soaked in 300ml (½ pint) boiling water
275g (10oz) Puy lentils, washed
Ground black pepper
450g (1lb) reduced-fat pork sausages

1 Fry the bacon in a non-stick saucepan until crisp, about 3 minutes. Add the vegetables, garlic and herbs and continue to cook until the vegetables have softened, about 5 minutes, adding a dash of water if necessary to prevent sticking.

2 Pour in the chicken stock and bring to the boil. Drain the ceps, but reserve the liquor. Squeeze the ceps dry and chop roughly, then add to the saucepan.

3 Pass the cep liquor through muslin into the saucepan. Add the lentils and cook for 20–30 minutes. If the lentils dry out too quickly, add some extra stock. The lentils should be wet but not soupy. Season with black pepper.

4 Meanwhile, skin the sausages and shape into eight flat patties. Grill the patties under a preheated grill, until golden and cooked through on both sides. For an easier version, simply grill the sausages.

5 Serve with the lentils and a green vegetable such as broccoli.

Per portion: 489 kcal, 8g fat, 2.6g sat fat, 0.69g sodium, 64g carbohydrate

pork with ale, black pepper and prunes

This is wonderful winter food. Marinating the pork and then slow cooking it on the hob and then in the oven infuses this casserole with rich, caramelised flavour. Serve with new potatoes in their skins and a green vegetable such as broccoli or cabbage.

SERVES 4

2 teaspoons black peppercorns, crushed
1 teaspoon dried oregano
1 teaspoon fresh thyme leaves
2 garlic cloves, crushed
1 tablespoon raw cane sugar
1 tablespoon wine vinegar
4 pork shoulder steaks, each weighing 125g (4½oz)
10g (½oz) butter
1 onion, finely sliced
1 tablespoon cornflour
200ml (7fl oz) strong ale
200ml (7fl oz) chicken stock
12 stoned prunes, halved

1 For the marinade, combine the crushed peppercorns, herbs, garlic, sugar and vinegar.

2 Rub the pork with the marinade, cover and leave to marinate in a cool place for at least 3 hours or overnight.

3 Preheat the oven to 180°C/350°F/gas mark 4.

4 Melt the butter in a flameproof casserole and cook the onion over a gentle heat until it is lightly golden. Set the pork on top of the onion slices in the casserole and lightly brown on both sides. Mix the cornflour with a little of the ale and add to the pan, then add the rest of the ale and the stock and bring just to a simmer. Add the prunes.

5 Cover, transfer to oven and cook for about 1 hour until tender.

Per portion: 274 kcal, 8g fat, 3.6g sat fat, 0.41g sodium, 21g carbohydrate

spaghetti bolognese

There are many ways to make spag bol – you can vary the herbs and vegetables, depending on what you have in your storecupboard, or for a vegetarian version, swap the beef and chicken livers for a selection of beans.

SERVES 6

50g (2oz) back bacon, diced
1 onion, finely diced
1 stick of celery, finely diced
1 carrot, finely diced
2 garlic cloves, crushed
1 teaspoon fresh soft thyme leaves
1 bay leaf
1 teaspoon dried oregano
400g (14oz) tin of chopped tomatoes
1 tablespoon tomato purée
1 tablespoon Worcestershire sauce
Ground black pepper
350g (12oz) extra-lean minced beef (coarsely ground, if possible)
1 teaspoon olive oil
100g (3^1/2oz) chicken livers
200ml (7fl oz/^{1}/4 bottle) dry red wine
600ml (1 pint) beef stock
500g (18oz) dried spaghetti
Freshly grated parmesan, to garnish (optional)

1 Heat a large, heavy-based saucepan and tip in the bacon. Cook for a couple of minutes until it is crispy and has released some natural fats, then add the onion, celery, carrot, garlic, thyme, bay leaf and oregano and cook over a medium heat until the vegetables have softened and taken on a little colour, stirring occasionally. Add a dash of water if necessary to prevent sticking.

2 Add the tinned tomatoes, tomato purée and Worcestershire sauce. Stir to combine and season with black pepper to taste.

3 Meanwhile, heat a large non-stick frying pan and fry the minced beef in small batches until browned. While the meat is frying, use a wooden spoon to break up any lumps. Repeat until all the beef is browned. Drain off any fat and stir the meat into the tomato mixture.

4 Wipe out the pan with some kitchen paper and add the oil, then fry the chicken livers until sizzling and lightly browned. Pour into the minced beef mixture, then deglaze the frying pan with some of the red wine, scraping any sediment from the bottom. Pour this wine, along with the rest of the wine and the stock into the minced beef mixture, stirring to combine.

5 Bring to the boil, then reduce the heat and simmer, uncovered, stirring from time to time, for about 1 hour until the beef is completely tender and the sauce is rich.

6 To serve, bring a large pan of water to a rolling boil. Swirl in the spaghetti, stir once and cook for 8–12 minutes or according to packet instructions until the pasta is *al dente*. Drain and divide among serving bowls. Pour over the sauce, scatter some parmesan, if using, and serve immediately.

Per portion: 471 kcal, 7g fat, 2.4g sat fat, 0.66g sodium, 68g carbohydrate

paprika goulash

A deliciously rich casserole with a spicy sweetness from the paprika and caraway. Serve with noodles and a green vegetable such as cabbage, green beans or broccoli.

SERVES 6

2 tablespoons cornflour
750g (1lb 10oz) chuck steak, brisket or silverside, cut into
    4cm (1¹/2in) pieces
1 tablespoon sunflower oil
50g (2oz) back bacon, chopped
3 garlic cloves, finely chopped
450g (1lb) onions, grated
1 tablespoon caraway seeds
1 tablespoon hot smoked paprika, plus extra for garnish
600ml (1 pint) beef stock
2 tablespoons tomato purée
Ground black pepper
1–2 x 150g (5oz) tubs 0% fat Greek-style yogurt

1 Tip the cornflour and beef into a plastic bag, seal the top and shake well until all the beef pieces are lightly dusted.

2 Heat the sunflower oil in a flameproof casserole, add the bacon, garlic, onions, caraway and paprika and cook for 3 minutes.

3 Add the beef to the pan, followed by the stock and tomato purée. Season with black pepper. Bring to a simmer, then cover and cook very gently for 2 hours, stirring occasionally, until the meat is tender and the sauce is reduced to a rich consistency.

4 Serve with a dollop of yogurt sprinkled with paprika.

Per portion: 274 kcal, 8g fat, 2.4g sat fat, 0.38g sodium, 16g carbohydrate

pot-roasted guinea fowl

Game birds contain very little fat, but that means that they dry out easily. This recipe is a great way to avoid that. Serve with green cabbage and new potatoes in their skins or sweet potato.

SERVES 8

2 sprigs of rosemary
2 sprigs of thyme
2 x 1.1kg (2¹/₂lb) guinea fowl or pheasant
Ground black pepper
10g (¹/₂oz) unsalted butter
1 tablespoon olive oil
4 slices back bacon, diced
1 large carrot, sliced
1 large onion, chopped
1 stick of celery, sliced
1 teaspoon soft thyme leaves
250ml (9fl oz) dry white wine
425ml (³/₄ pint) chicken stock

1 Preheat the oven to 220°C/425°F/gas mark 7.

2 Place the rosemary and thyme in the cavity of the birds. Season the birds with pepper.

3 In a deep flameproof casserole, brown the birds in the butter and olive oil until golden all over. Remove and set aside.

4 To the same casserole, add the bacon, carrot, onion, celery and thyme. Cook until the vegetables have softened and started to brown. Add the wine, scraping any coagulated sediment from the bottom of the pan.

5 Return the birds to the casserole, pour in the chicken stock and bring to a simmer. Cover with a lid and place in the oven. Cook for 1–1¹/₂ hours until the thickest part of the thighs is tender when tested with a skewer.

Per portion: 289 kcal, 7g fat, 5.1g sat fat, 0.42g sodium, 4g carbohydrate

fillet steak with salsa verde

A good steak is mouthwatering, but we have become more wary of red meat. Try to buy organic, ensure each portion size is no bigger than 125g (4½oz) and you can still enjoy it occasionally. Serve with boiled new potatoes in their skins and green beans.

SERVES 4

Small handful flat-leaf parsley
6 basil leaves
¹/₂ small handful mint leaves
1 pickled cucumber
1 garlic clove
1 tablespoon capers, drained and rinsed
2 anchovy fillets, rinsed
¹/₂ tablespoon red wine vinegar
¹/₂ tablespoon fresh lemon juice
¹/₂ tablespoon Dijon mustard
3 tablespoons extra-virgin olive oil
Ground black pepper
4 x 125g (4¹/₂oz) fillet steaks

1 Coarsely chop the parsley, basil, mint and cucumber with the garlic, capers and anchovy fillets, or pulse in a food-processor but you will get a better result if you chop by hand.

2 Transfer to a non-metallic bowl and whisk in the red wine vinegar, lemon juice, Dijon mustard, all but 1 teaspoon of the olive oil, plus 2 tablespoons cold water. Season with pepper. Set aside, covered with clingfilm, at room temperature.

3 Heat a heavy-based frying pan or ridged grill pan. Brush the steaks with the remaining oil and cook for 2–3 minutes on each side, depending on how rare you like your steak.

4 Transfer the steak to a plate and set aside in a warm place for about 5 minutes. Serve with some salsa verde on the side.

Per portion: 279 kcal, 18g fat, 4.7g sat fat, 0.49g sodium, 1g carbohydrate

crispy duck with lentils

Although duck contains quite a lot of fat, draining it as it cooks will reduce your intake.

SERVES 6

3 large duck breast fillets
1¹/2 teaspoons ground cumin or cinnamon

Lentils
350g (12oz) Puy lentils, washed but not soaked
1 onion, finely chopped
1 bay leaf
1 whole clove
1 carrot, diced
100g (3¹/2oz) back bacon, cut in strips
Few sprigs of thyme
2 garlic cloves, peeled
600ml (1 pint) chicken stock
1 teaspoon raw cane sugar
Ground black pepper

1 To make the lentils, place them in a saucepan and cover with cold water. Bring to the boil, drain and rinse under cold water. Return the lentils to the saucepan and add the onion, bay leaf, clove, carrot, bacon, thyme, garlic, chicken stock and sugar. Bring to the boil, then reduce the heat, cover the pan, and simmer until the lentils are tender but not mushy, about 20 minutes, adding water as necessary. Drain the lentils if preferred but discard the bay leaf, clove, thyme and garlic. Season with black pepper and keep warm.

2 Meanwhile, cut the skin of the duck in a very close criss-cross pattern and dust with the spice. Place skin side down in a heavy-based frying pan over a medium heat and cook for 10 minutes until the skin is crisp. Pour off any excess fat. Turn the duck skin side up, and cook for a further 5–10 minutes to suit your taste. Leave to rest for 5 minutes then slice thickly.

3 Pile the lentils onto plates and top with the duck slices.

Per portion: 355 kcal, 8g fat, 2.4g sat fat, 0.54g sodium, 37g carbohydrate

roast turkey

This is a great way to roast a turkey without running the risk of drying the meat, as the herby butter and cheese pushed under the skin baste the turkey as it cooks. See page 124 for another way to roast poultry.

SERVES 16

110g (4oz) ricotta or low-fat soft cheese
50g (2oz) unsalted butter, softened
1 tablespoon snipped chives
1 tablespoon chopped flat-leaf parsley
1 tablespoon chopped tarragon
1/2 teaspoon sea salt
1/2 teaspoon ground black pepper
4.4kg (10lb) fresh turkey, at room temperature
1 lemon, halved
1 onion, halved
3 garlic cloves
Sprig of thyme
Sprig of rosemary

1 Preheat the oven to 230°C/450°F/gas mark 8.

2 Combine the ricotta and butter with the chopped herbs, salt and pepper.

3 Gently ease the skin covering the turkey breast away from the flesh at both ends by carefully inserting your fingers between the skin and flesh. Push the cheese mixture under the skin, easing it over the whole bird, being careful not to puncture the skin. Place the lemon, onion, garlic and herbs in the cavity of the turkey.

4 Lay a large sheet of non-stick foil in a roasting tin lengthways, leaving enough at each end to wrap over the turkey. Repeat this exercise with another sheet, this time across the roasting tray.

5 Place the turkey breast side up in the centre of the foil. Wrap the turkey completely in foil and roast for 2 hours. Fold back the foil, making sure the ends of the drumsticks are still covered. Baste the turkey with the juices that have formed in the tin, then cook for a further 30 minutes until the turkey is golden brown. Check with a metal skewer to see if the turkey is cooked – the juices in the thickest part of the thigh should run clear.

6 Remove from the oven and allow to rest in a warm place for 15 minutes to allow the juices to settle and to ease carving. Carefully skim off the fat from the roasting tray and use the remaining meat juices to make gravy, if liked.

Per portion: 295 kcal, 13g fat, 5.1g sat fat, 0.21g sodium, 1g carbohydrate

kofta meatballs

This is a fragrant Middle Eastern dish where minced meat is flavoured with spices and formed into balls. They also freeze well and makes a great snack for kids.

SERVES 4

500g (18oz) extra-lean beef or lamb, finely minced
1 onion, finely chopped
2 teaspoons ground cumin
1 teaspoon ground mixed spice
Pinch of cayenne pepper
Handful of chopped coriander leaves
Ground black pepper
1 tablespoon olive oil
Lemon wedges, to serve

1 Blend all the ingredients except the oil in a food-processor until smooth.

2 Take a small handful of the mixture and, using your hands, roll it into a ball or oval shape. Repeat until you have used all the mixture to make 16 meatballs. If you wet your hands first, it will help prevent the mixture from sticking to them.

3 Heat the oil in a large non-stick frying pan and fry the meatballs until they are golden brown and cooked through. Drain on absorbent kitchen paper and serve with lemon wedges. They are delicious with a green salad and couscous or brown rice.

Per portion: 212 kcal, 9g fat, 3.2g sat fat, 0.08g sodium, 4g carbohydrate

black pudding with apples

Black pudding is one of the oldest kinds of sausage in Europe. Love or hate it, it is a good source of iron.

SERVES 4

250g (9oz or 8–12 slices) black pudding (preferably a soft
   variety), cut into 1cm (1/2in) slices
2 shallots, finely chopped
1 tablespoon walnut oil
2 pink-skinned dessert apples, e.g. Pink Lady or Cox, cored
   and cut into thin slices
4 tablespoons chopped parsley
1 tablespoon cider vinegar
Ground black pepper

Crushed white beans
250g (9oz) white beans
1 onion, roughly chopped
1 carrot, chopped
1 stick of celery, chopped
2 teaspoons chopped garlic
50g (2oz) ham, roughly chopped
1 clove
Sprig of thyme
1 bay leaf
1/2 tablespoon ground cumin
1/2 teaspoon ground chilli powder

1 To make the white beans, soak them overnight in cold water.

2 Rinse the beans then place in a large pan with the onion, carrot, celery, garlic, ham, clove, thyme and bay leaf.

3 Cover with cold water, bring to the boil and simmer until the beans are soft (approximately 1 hour), adding more water if necessary to keep the beans covered. Drain the beans and remove the clove, thyme and bay leaf.

4 Crush the beans with a potato masher then mix in the ground cumin and chilli powder.

5 Preheat the grill to medium and cook the black pudding slices for 2 minutes each side. The slices should be slightly crusty. Remove and set aside, discarding any tough skin.

6 Heat the oil in a medium frying pan and cook the shallots over a medium heat until soft but not brown. Add the apple, cook for a further 2 minutes, then add the parsley.

7 Pour in the cider vinegar and combine with the other ingredients. Season to taste with pepper.

8 Warm through the bean purée and spoon onto warmed plates. Top with slices of black pudding and garnish with the apple mixture. Serve immediately.

Per portion: 343 kcal, 18g fat, 5.8g sat fat, 0.74g sodium, 33g carbohydrate

shepherd's pie with a gi twist

The bean mash reduces the GI and the herbs and chilli liven up what can be quite a heavy dish. If you prefer to make this in advance and reheat from cold, then allow about 45 minutes in an oven preheated to 220°C/425°F/gas mark 7.

SERVES 6

600g (1¼lb) lean lamb, coarsely minced
Ground black pepper
2 onions, finely chopped
2 carrots, diced
2 sticks of celery, finely sliced
½ teaspoon ground cinnamon
½ teaspoon thyme leaves
½ teaspoon chopped rosemary
25g (1oz) cornflour
4 teaspoons tomato purée
2 teaspoons Worcestershire sauce
300ml (½ pint) red wine
200ml (7fl oz) lamb or chicken stock

Bean mash
2 tablespoons extra-virgin olive oil
5 garlic cloves
2 sprigs of fresh rosemary
1 large dried chilli
3 x 400g (14oz) tins of cannellini beans, drained and rinsed
About 300ml (½ pint) chicken stock
8 tablespoons coarsely chopped flat-leaf parsley
6 spring onions, finely sliced
1 teaspoon very finely chopped rosemary
Ground black pepper

1 Season the lamb with pepper. Heat a large non-stick saucepan and when hot add the lamb and brown the meat – it will probably need to be done in batches. You only want to brown the meat, not cook it.

2 Drain each batch of lamb over a bowl and set aside. Once the fat in the bowl has coagulated, reserve 2 teaspoons and

any meat juices. Wipe out the pan and add the 2 teaspoons fat and the vegetables and season with pepper and cinnamon. Then add the chopped herbs. Cook for 8 minutes until the vegetables begin to soften.

3 Add the lamb and cook on a medium heat for a few minutes. Add the cornflour, tomato purée and Worcestershire sauce. Stir to combine everything thoroughly.

4 Add the red wine, a third at a time, reducing the liquid by three-quarters after each addition. Pour in the stock, the reserved meat juices and about 300m (½ pint) water and bring to a simmer.

5 Cook for about 1 hour. If the sauce becomes too thick during the cooking time add a little extra water, but remember you don't want the mixture to be too thin. During the last 30 minutes of cooking make the bean mash.

6 To make the mash, pour the oil into a saucepan over a low heat. Add the garlic, rosemary and chilli and cook until the garlic and chilli are golden in colour. Discard the garlic, rosemary and chilli and keep the oil warm.

7 Meanwhile heat the beans in the chicken stock (you want enough stock just to cover the beans). Cook until the beans are hot but not boiling. Drain, retaining the liquor. Place half the beans in a food-processor and blend until smooth. With the machine running, add the warm oil. With a rubber spatula scrape the purée into a bowl and fold in the whole beans and the remaining ingredients with enough stock to give a spreadable consistency. Season with black pepper to taste.

8 Once the shepherd's mince is ready, ladle it into a large ovenproof dish, level out the top and spoon the bean mash over the top. Finish the pie in a very hot oven (220°C/425°F/gas mark 7) for 15–20 minutes or under a preheated grill to become slightly golden.

Per portion: 411 kcal, 14g fat, 4.5g sat fat, 0.41g sodium, 11g carbohydrate

barley 'risotto'

Here I used pearl barley instead of arborio rice, which has a high GI. This also means there is much less stirring!

SERVES: 4–6

10g (1/2oz) unsalted butter

2 leeks, sliced and rinsed

2 garlic cloves, finely chopped

1/2 teaspoon soft thyme leaves

350g (12oz) pearl barley or brown wholegrain barley

1/2 teaspoon cayenne pepper

About 1.2 litres (2 pints) chicken stock

110g (4oz) chorizo sausage, diced

2 handfuls of mixed spinach and rocket

4 tablespoons chopped flat-leaf parsley

2 tablespoons snipped chives

25g (1oz) freshly grated parmesan

1 Melt the butter in a large saucepan over a medium heat. Add the leeks, garlic and thyme. Cook for 3–4 minutes until the leeks have started to soften, adding a dash of water if necessary to prevent sticking.

2 Stir in the barley, cayenne and chicken stock. Bring to the boil, reduce the heat and simmer, covered, until the liquid has evaporated and the barley is tender, adding a little extra stock as necessary – this should take about 40 minutes.

3 Add the chorizo, spinach and rocket and stir through until the leaves have just wilted.

4 Sprinkle with the herbs and serve topped with the parmesan.

Per portion: 498 kcal, 14g fat, 5.7g sat fat, 0.71g sodium, 80g carbohydrate

puddings

cherry bread pudding

There are many variations on this bread pudding – try using different fruits.

SERVES 6–8

600ml (1 pint) semi-skimmed milk
1 vanilla pod, split
3 eggs
50g (2oz) golden caster sugar
6 thick slices wholegrain bread, crusts removed
9 tablespoons cherry spread
50g (2oz) dried cherries

1 Bring the milk to the boil with the vanilla pod.

2 Whisk the eggs and sugar and pour the milk over. Scrape the seeds from the vanilla pod into the custard.

3 Cover the bread with cherry spread and cut in quarters. Arrange in a shallow baking dish and strain the egg and milk mixture over. Sprinkle with the cherries and leave to soak for about 2 hours.

4 Preheat the oven to 160°C/325°F/gas mark 3. Cook the pudding in a hot bain-marie for 25–30 minutes until just set. Serve warm.

Per portion: 383 kcal, 7g fat, 2.3g sat fat, 0.53g sodium, 72g carbohydrate

summer pudding

This is a classic English pudding, using summer berries such as redcurrants, raspberries and blackcurrants, but you could use any kind of berry, including blackberries. Save a few berries to decorate the pudding.

SERVES 8

900g (2lb) raspberries
225g (8oz) redcurrants, picked over
50g (2oz) blackcurrants, picked over
125g (4^1/2oz) golden caster sugar
10–12 slices of day-old wholegrain bread, crusts removed
125ml (4fl oz) cherry brandy
Extra berries, to decorate

1 Sprinkle the fruit with the sugar and toss gently to combine. Cover and leave to macerate for 2 hours.

2 Meanwhile line a 1.8 litre (3 pint) pudding basin with cling film then with slices of bread. Make sure the bread overlaps slightly and covers the sides and bottom completely.

3 Tip the fruit and resulting juices into a non-reactive saucepan with the cherry brandy and cook over a medium heat for 3–4 minutes to release some more juices.

4 Using a slotted spoon, fill up the bread mould with fruit. Pour over half the juices, then cover the fruit completely with more bread slices. Cover with clingfilm, then top with a plate that fits into the rim of the bowl. Place a heavy weight on top of the plate and refrigerate overnight.

5 When ready to serve, turn the bowl over onto a shallow, but not flat dish and remove the bowl and clingfilm. Pour over the reserved juices and serve with a few loose berries.

Per portion: 263 kcal, 2g fat, 0.4g sat fat, 0.32g sodium, 52g carbohydrate

pear crumble

This has a very fine textured topping which absorbs the delicious juices from the pears, citrus zest and nutmeg.

SERVES 6–8

8 ripe Conference pears, peeled, cored and sliced
Finely grated zest of 1 orange and 1 lemon
2 tablespoons golden caster sugar
Pinch of grated nutmeg
25g (1oz) reduced-fat powdered milk
25g (1oz) ground almonds
50g (2oz) porridge oats
175g (6oz) wholegrain plain flour
110g (4oz) soft dark brown sugar
1 teaspoon ground cinnamon
40g (1¹/₂oz) unsalted butter, softened

1 Preheat the oven to 200°C/400°F/gas mark 6.

2 Combine the pears with the zest, sugar, nutmeg and 100ml (3¹/₂fl oz) water in the base of a large baking dish.

3 Mix the dry ingredients together then rub in the butter.

4 Pop this mixture on top of the pears and bake for 45 minutes to 1 hour, or until the top is golden. Serve warm with low-sugar custard.

Per portion (excluding custard): 433 kcal, 10g fat, 3.8g sat fat, 0.04g sodium, 85g carbohydrate

drunken berries

Macerating fruit in spirits and sugar softens them and fills them with lovely flavours. Berries have a low GI and are packed full of vitamins, so this is an easy, virtually fat-free way to enjoy them.

SERVES 4–6

1 punnet (225g/8oz) strawberries, hulled and quartered
1 punnet (175g/6oz) raspberries, picked over
1 punnet (150g/5oz) blackberries, picked over
1 punnet (150g/5oz) redcurrants, berries removed from
*   their stems*
4 tablespoons crème de cassis
1 tablespoon icing sugar
1 tablespoon lemon juice (optional)

1 In a glass bowl combine all the fruits gently with the cassis, icing sugar and lemon juice, if using. Allow to macerate for approximately 3 hours, turning the fruits from time to time.

2 Serve on their own or with low-fat natural yogurt.

Per portion: 124 kcal, 0.3g fat, 0.0g sat fat, 0.01g sodium, 23g carbohydrate

whole poached apricots

Typically Mediterranean, this is also incredibly easy to make. To remove the stones from fresh apricots, just make a small cut and the stone will come out easily – don't cut the apricots all the way through. If you can't find fresh apricots, you could use dried apricots, but halve the weight and soak for several hours in cold water until plump.

SERVES 6

75g (3oz) golden caster sugar
4 green cardamom pods, crushed
2 teaspoons fresh lemon juice
1kg (2¹/4lb) ripe apricots, split, stone removed
50g (2oz) flaked almonds or pine nuts, toasted
Pomegranate seeds (optional)

1 Preheat the oven to 180°C/350°F/gas mark 4.

2 Pour 600ml (1 pint) water into a wide flameproof dish with the sugar, cardamom and lemon juice and bring to the boil. When boiling, add the apricots and remove from the heat. Cover them with wet parchment paper, put the lid on the dish and place in the oven. Cook for 20–30 minutes. Remove from the oven and allow to cool in the syrup.

3 To serve, remove the apricots and drain, reserving the syrup. Top with the flaked toasted almonds and pomegranate seeds, if using and pour over some of the syrup.

Per portion: 153 kcal, 5g fat, 0.4g sat fat, 0.01g sodium, 26g carbohydrate

compôte of plums in spiced rosemary syrup

This is luscious. Very like mulled wine, but with plums, all the flavours intensify and combine to make a lovely thick syrup.

SERVES 4

150ml (¹/4 pint) red wine
50g (2oz) caster sugar
Sprig of rosemary
1 bay leaf
1 strip each lemon and orange zest
2 whole cloves
5cm (2in) piece of cinnamon stick
500g (18oz) red plums, halved and stoned

1 Bring the first seven ingredients to the boil and simmer until the sugar has dissolved. Add the plums and cover with a lid. Cook gently until the plums are just tender.

2 Remove the plums and set aside. If wished, boil the juices to reduce slightly. Pour over the plums and serve warm or cold with low-fat natural yogurt.

Per portion: 125 kcal, 0.2g fat, 0.0g sat fat, 0.01g sodium, 25g carbohydrate

rice pudding

Rice puddings have to be cooked slowly for best results, but it is comfort food for all the family. If you are using brown short-grain rice, cover it with cold water and bring to the boil. Reduce the heat and simmer for 15 minutes, then drain and continue as above. You will also need more rice – 125g (4½oz) – and to cook it for longer – 2–3 hours.

SERVES 4–6

75g (3oz) short-grain rice
Pinch of salt
50g (2 oz) golden caster sugar
850ml–1.2 litres (1½–2 pints) skimmed milk
Grated nutmeg or cinnamon
25g (1oz) butter

1 Preheat the oven to 150°C/300°F/gas mark 2.

2 Wash and drain the rice and put in a 1.4–1.7 litre (2½–3 pint) baking dish.

3 Add a pinch of salt, the sugar and 850ml (1½ pints) milk, and stir. Sprinkle grated nutmeg or cinnamon over and top with knobs of butter. Bake in the centre or towards the bottom of the oven for about 2 hours. Stir in the skin that forms on the top at least once during the cooking time, adding extra milk as necessary.

Per portion: 235 kcal, 6g fat, 3.9g sat fat, 0.25g sodium, 39g carbohydrate

baked peaches

Peaches are just as good cooked as they are fresh. This is a really simple recipe, but it looks wonderful when it comes out of the oven.

SERVES 4

Juice of 1 lime
Pinch of grated nutmeg
2 tablespoons soft brown sugar
25g (1oz) unsalted butter, softened
25g (1oz) chopped toasted hazelnuts
4 ripe peaches (yellow or white), halved and stone removed

1 Preheat the oven to 190°C/375°F/gas mark 5.

2 Mix together the lime juice, nutmeg, sugar, butter and hazelnuts.

3 Place the peaches, cut side up, in a baking dish in which they fit snugly and divide the sugar mixture between the peach halves. Bake for about 20 minutes until the syrup is bubbling and there are golden-brown flecks on the peaches. Baste the peaches occasionally with the syrupy juices that come from them while they are cooking. Serve warm.

Per portion: 160 kcal, 9g fat, 3.6g sat fat, 0.01g sodium, 19g carbohydrate

baked apples with fruit and nuts

Small Bramleys are perfect for this dish as they cook to a soft purée encased in lightly caramelised skins. Large dessert apples could also be used.

SERVES 4

4 small Bramley cooking apples, each weighing about
   225g (8oz)
25g (1oz) soft dark brown sugar
4 tablespoons sweet mincemeat
25g (1oz) flaked almonds or chopped pecans
1 teaspoon ground cinnamon
Butter, for greasing
About 150ml (1/4 pint) apple juice for basting

1 Preheat the oven to 190°C/375°F/gas mark 5.

2 Remove the centre core from the apples, leaving 5mm (1/4in) uncut at the bottom. Run the tip of a sharp knife round the circumference of the apple, just to pierce the skin – this will stop the apples bursting in the oven.

3 Combine the remaining ingredients except the juice and press into the cavities of the apples. Place them in a buttered baking dish in which they fit snugly, then pour in 2 tablespoons apple juice and pop in the oven for 45 minutes to 1 hour. At 10-minute intervals, add 2 more tablespoons apple juice to the bottom of the dish and spoon the juices over the apples. Serve warm.

Per portion: 251 kcal, 5g fat, 0.3g sat fat, 0.02g sodium, 53g carbohydrate

herby fruit salad

A twist on a classic fruit salad, the Asian influence of coriander and coconut milk is unusual yet refreshing – perfect after a heavy meal.

SERVES 4–6

4 tablespoons reduced-fat coconut milk
1 tablespoon liquid honey
Lemon or lime juice, to taste
2 blood oranges or small pink grapefruit, peeled and sliced
1 small pineapple, peeled and diced
1 pink-skinned apple, cored and diced
1 banana, peeled and sliced
1 small mango, peeled and diced
2 tablespoons chopped coriander leaves

Mix the coconut milk, honey and lemon juice. Toss the fruits and coriander in this dressing.

Per portion: 141 kcal, 0.5g fat, 0.1g sat fat, 0.02g sodium, 34g carbohydrate

sauces and accompaniments

rich tomato sauce

This is an excellent recipe that can be used as a base for many dishes. Or serve it with gnocchi or wholewheat pasta.

SERVES 6–8 – MAKES ABOUT 800ML (SCANT 1¹/₂ PINTS)

1 tablespoon extra-virgin olive oil
1 onion, finely diced
2 garlic cloves, finely diced
1 stick of celery, finely diced
150ml (¹/₄ pint) dry white wine
750g (1lb 10oz) plum tomatoes, peeled, de-seeded and
    diced, or 2 x 400g (14oz) tins of chopped tomatoes
1 fresh bay leaf
1 teaspoon tomato purée
Handful of roughly chopped fresh herbs, such as flat-leaf
    parsley, marjoram and basil
Ground black pepper

1 Heat a heavy-based saucepan and add the olive oil, then stir in the onion, garlic and celery and cook for about 5 minutes until soften but not coloured, stirring occasionally. Pour in the wine and allow to bubble away, then add the tomatoes with the bay leaf and tomato purée.

2 Bring the sauce to the boil, then simmer gently, uncovered, for about 30 minutes, stirring occasionally until the sauce is well reduced and thickened. Remove from the heat and leave to cool a little.

3 When the sauce has cooled, remove the bay leaf and stir in the herbs. Season to taste with black pepper and reheat gently to use as required.

Per 100ml: 36 kcal, 1g fat, 0.2g sat fat, 0.01g sodium, 7g carbohydrate

parsley sauce

A classic recipe that is great with fish or vegetables.

SERVES 4 – MAKES 300ML (¹/₂ PINT)

10g (¹/₂oz) unsalted butter
2 tablespoons cornflour
350–450ml (12–16fl oz) skimmed milk
3 tablespoons chopped parsley
Handful of fresh sorrel leaves, shredded (optional)
Ground white pepper

1 Melt the butter in a small pan. Add the cornflour, stirring. Pour in the milk, a little at a time, beating vigorously until smooth after each addition. Simmer gently for 2–3 minutes until smooth and thickened, stirring occasionally.

2 Add the parsley and sorrel, if using, and reheat gently until the sorrel has just wilted. Season with white pepper to taste.

Per 100ml: 72 kcal, 2g fat, 1.2g sat fat, 0.04g sodium, 14g carbohydrate

red onion marmalade

Tasty with cheese or cold meats, spread a little onto a crostini before topping with other ingredients. If you like, you can use white onions, white wine and white wine vinegar, but add raisins instead of prunes. This makes a great gift.

SERVES 10 – MAKES ABOUT 500ML (18FL OZ)

25g (1oz) unsalted butter
750g (1lb 10oz) red onions, thinly sliced
1/2 teaspoon rock salt
1 bay leaf
1 teaspoon soft thyme leaves
1/2 teaspoon ground black pepper
50g (2oz) golden caster sugar
1 tablespoon dry sherry
1 tablespoon aged red wine vinegar
200ml (7fl oz) red wine
1 tablespoon liquid honey
50g (2oz) pitted prunes, chopped

1 Melt the butter in a heavy-based saucepan over a medium heat. Add the onions, salt, bay leaf, thyme and pepper. Stir to combine. Reduce the heat, cover and cook for about 30 minutes, stirring from time to time, and adding a splash of water if it starts to stick.

2 Remove the lid and add the remaining ingredients. Cook over a very low heat until it becomes dark in colour, about 45 minutes. Keep a look out for burning towards the end of cooking. Stir regularly.

3 Cool and store in sterilised glass jars, refrigerated. This will keep for 2 months.

Per 100g: 83 kcal, 2g fat, 1.2g sat fat, 0.09g sodium, 15g carbohydrate

coriander mint chutney

Delicious as chutney, this also makes a great dip if you fold it into low-fat natural yogurt. Eat with poppadoms and tandoori dishes.

MAKES 150ML (1/4 PINT)

25g (1oz) mint leaves
40g (11/2oz) coriander leaves
1/2 small onion, roughly chopped
1cm (1/2in) fresh ginger, peeled and chopped
1/2 chilli, de-seeded and roughly chopped
1/4 teaspoon cumin seeds
1 small garlic clove
1/2 teaspoon salt
1/2 tablespoon lemon juice
1/2 tablespoon desiccated coconut, moistened in
   1/2 tablespoon water

Blend all the ingredients in a food-processor until well combined. It will keep for a few days if you store in an airtight container in the refrigerator.

Per 100ml: 73 kcal, 5g fat, 3.8g sat fat, 0.56g sodium, 8g carbohydrate

pickled blackberries

A pickle that goes well with cheese or cold meats such as duck. Blackberries are also a superfruit as they contain so much goodness – the antioxidant vitamins C and E as well as fibre. They also have a lovely rich colour.

SERVES 10

500g (18oz) blackberries
250g (9oz) golden caster sugar
1 teaspoon ground allspice
1 tablespoon ground ginger
150ml (¼ pint) white wine vinegar

1 In a bowl, combine the blackberries, sugar and spices, stir through, cover and leave to marinate overnight.

2 Bring the vinegar to the boil, add the berries and simmer gently, uncovered, for 20 minutes.

3 Allow to cool and spoon into sterilised jars. This will keep for a couple of months in the fridge.

Per 100g: 118 kcal, 0.1g fat, 0.0g sat fat, 0.01g sodium, 28g carbohydrate

sweet pickled onions

The best pickling recipe I have tried, especially if you like your onions a little sweet. Salting is the first stage of this recipe, and although a large amount of salt is used here, a lot of it is discarded before pickling. Be warned, this needs to be made over a couple of days.

MAKES TWO LARGE JARS (APPROX 850ML/1½PINTS EACH)

1.1kg (2½lb) peeled pickling onions
50g (2oz) salt
110g (4oz) soft brown sugar
110g (4oz) golden syrup
1 teaspoon whole cloves
1 tablespoon black peppercorns
2 red chillies, quartered and de-seeded
Pinch of mustard seeds
5cm (2in) piece of cinnamon stick
1 bay leaf
Sprig of thyme
3 slices ginger
600ml (1 pint) malt vinegar

1 Mix the onions with the salt and leave overnight.

2 In a non-reactive saucepan, combine the sugar, golden syrup, cloves, peppercorns, chillies, mustard seeds, cinnamon, bay leaf, thyme, ginger and malt vinegar. Bring to the boil, remove from the heat and leave to cool overnight.

3 The next day, drain and dry the onions and pack into sterilised storage jars. Boil the pickling liquor and pour it over the onions, evenly distributing the herbs and spices.

4 Seal the jars and store for 2 weeks before eating. Once opened, they will keep for several months in the fridge.

Per 100g: 54 kcal, 0.1g fat, 0.0g sat fat, 1.00g sodium, 12g carbohydrate

Index

acknowledgements

There are too many people to thank but certain individuals deserve a special mention:

To my wonderful wife, Jacinta and our two children, Toby and Billie, who suffered from my lack of quality time yet supported me throughout as I managed to juggle my time through two books and everything else going on in my life.

To Louise, my energetic and ultra-efficient PA, who fielded hundreds of phone calls from the publishers and who was regularly on hand to smooth troubled waters when the pressures of deadlines occasionally took their toll.

To Fiona Lindsay, Linda Shanks and Lesley Turnbull at Limelight Management who are constantly there to make sure I have more than enough work to handle.

To my team at Notting Grill and Kew Grill, especially David, George, Antonio and Candido, who kept the boat afloat in my often extended absences.

To the various friends Nicki, Kate, Sarah, John and Anne, June, Mike and Nicky who acted unknowingly as guinea pigs for many of the recipes.

To Dr Mabel Blades for her guidance on the GI and Jane Suthering for her creativity in helping to make my recipes GI-friendly.

And finally to Muna Reyal, my editor and her fab team at Kyle Cathie, for giving me the opportunity to produce this cookbook. They turned my offerings into a beautifully executed book.
(Antony Worrall Thompson)

I would like to thank my husband, Peter Blades, for his love and encouragement as well as for helping me to keep the midnight oil burning. And thanks also to Daisy Rose, my long-time Australian friend for her great interest and support.

I have also really enjoyed working with Antony and Jane, especially as we all spoke the same language about food, and I would like to thank my editor, Muna, for holding my hand throughout and giving us cakes and wine in the office.
(Mabel Blades)

As ever creating a book is all about team work – and what a great team it's been. We've prepared and tasted every recipe – as many as 7 in a day sometimes – and even so I've still managed to lose a few pounds in weight. I'm certainly a GI convert!
(Jane Suthering)

bibliography

Nutrition and Health
by Mabel Blades
Highfield Books

The New Glucose Revolution
by Anthony Leeds, Jennie Brand-Miller, Kaye Foster-Powell and Stephen Colagiuri
Hodder Mobius

The GI Point Diet
by Azmina Govindji and Nina Puddefoot
Vermilion

Healthy Eating for Diabetes
by Antony Worrall Thompson and Azmina Govindji
Kyle Cathie Ltd